Mastering Global
Corporate Governance

Mastering Global Corporate Governance

Editor

Ulrich Steger

John Wiley & Sons, Ltd

Other Wiley Editorial Offices

John Wiley & Sons Inc., 111 River Street, Hoboken, NJ 07030, USA

Jossey-Bass, 989 Market Street, San Francisco, CA 94103-1741, USA

Wiley-VCH Verlag GmbH, Boschstr. 12, D-69469 Weinheim, Germany

John Wiley & Sons Australia Ltd, 33 Park Road, Milton, Queensland 4064, Australia

John Wiley & Sons (Asia) Pte Ltd, 2 Clementi Loop #02-01, Jin Xing Distripark, Singapore 129809

John Wiley & Sons Canada Ltd, 22 Worcester Road, Etobicoke, Ontario, Canada M9W 1L1

Wiley also publishes its books in a variety of electronic formats. Some content that appears
in print may not be available in electronic books.

Library of Congress Cataloging-in-Publication Data

Mastering global corporate governance / editor Ulrich Steger ; contributing
authors Bill George . . . [et al.].
    p. cm.
  Includes bibliographical references.
  ISBN 0-470-09041-3
  1. Corporate governance. 2. International business
enterprises – Management. I. Steger, Ulrich. II. George, Bill (William W.)
  HD2741.M33 2004
  658'.049 – dc22

                                              2004000198

British Library Cataloguing in Publication Data

A catalogue record for this book is available from the British Library

ISBN 0-470-09041-3

Typeset in 10/16pt Kuenstler by Laserwords Private Limited, Chennai, India
Printed and bound in Great Britain by TJ International, Padstow, Cornwall
This book is printed on acid-free paper responsibly manufactured from sustainable forestry
in which at least two trees are planted for each one used for paper production.

Contents

Contributors

Bill George – Professor of Leadership and Governance, IMD

Bill George is Professor of Leadership and Governance at IMD and also Visiting Professor of Management at Ecole Polytechnique Fédérale Lausanne (EPFL). He was Chairman of the Board of Medtronic, the world's leading medical technology company, from 1996 to 2002 and Chief Executive Officer from 1991 to 2001, having joined Medtronic in 1989 as president.

He was named Director of the Year 2001–02 by the National Association of Corporate Directors and Executive of the Year 2001 by the Academy of Management. Mr George is a board member of Novartis and Target Corporations. He also serves as a director of American Red Cross, Harvard Business School, Carnegie Endowment, Allina Hospitals, Minneapolis Institute of Arts, and as Chair of Minnesota Thunder Pro Soccer.

He was an executive with Honeywell from 1978 to 1989 and Litton Industries from 1969 to 1978. From 1966 to 1969 he worked in the US Department of Defense. He received his BSIE with high honors from Georgia Tech in 1964 and his MBA with high distinction from Harvard

Business School in 1966. His book, *Authentic Leadership*, was published by Jossey-Bass in 2003.

Helga Krapf – PhD student, University of Berlin

Helga Krapf is a researcher for the Global Corporate Governance Research Initiative. A doctoral student at the University of Berlin, she is writing her thesis on 'The Context and Shaping Factors for Investor Relations in Global Companies'.

Peter Lorange – President and The Nestlé Professor, IMD

Dr Peter Lorange has been the President of IMD since 1 July 1993. He is Professor of Strategy and holds the Nestlé Chair. He was formerly President of the Norwegian School of Management in Oslo. His areas of special interest are global strategic management, strategic planning and entrepreneurship for growth.

Dr Lorange has written or edited 13 books and some 90 articles. He has conducted extensive research on multinational management, strategic planning processes, and internally generated growth processes. He has taught at the undergraduate, Master and Doctoral levels, and worked extensively within his areas of expertise with US, European and Asian corporations, both in a consulting capacity and in executive education.

He serves on the board of directors of several corporations including: ISS – International Service Systems, Christiania Eiendomsselskap, S. Ugel-stad Shipowners, StreamServe AB, Pharmasoft AB, Intentia International AB, and Preferred Global Health. He is also a board member of the Copen-hagen Business School.

Franz-Friedrich Neubauer – Professor of Multinational Corporate Strategy and Planning at IMD

Dr F. Friedrich Neubauer, Professor of Multinational Corporate Strategy and Planning at IMD, is German; he joined IMI, Geneva, one of the parent organizations of IMD, in 1973.

Fred Neubauer is author of several books (and numerous articles). *Portfolio Management*, originally published in German (1990), now appears in English, Slovenian and Spanish. His present research interests are concentrated in the areas of corporate boards and European management approaches. In the area of corporate boards he – together with Dr Ada Demb – has been involved in a large empirical study on boards. The results of the study were published by Oxford University Press in March 1992 (Demb/Neubauer, *The Corporate Board: Confronting the Paradoxes*). His latest book – *The Family Business: Its governance for sustainability* (Macmillan, 1998) – was published together with Alden G. Lank. It is based on a four-year study of governance issues in family businesses.

Dr Neubauer is also a consultant in the area of strategic management and corporate governance. In the course of his career he has advised a broad range of companies, among them several large multinational car makers, soft drink and fragrance corporations, internationally active banks, packaging equipment manufacturers, building material producers etc. He also conducts in-company board retreats where the whole board of a given company looks at its own performance as a board.

Ulrich Steger – Alcan Professor of Environment, IMD

Ulrich Steger holds the Alcan Chair of Environmental Management at IMD and is Director of IMD's research project on Corporate Sustainability

Management, CSM. He is also Director of all DaimlerChrysler Partnership Programs, the Allianz Excellence Program and the Yukos Program. In addition, Professor Steger heads IMD's Global Corporate Governance Research Initiative.

He is also a member of the supervisory and advisory boards of several major companies and organizations. He was a member of the managing board of Volkswagen, in charge of environment and traffic matters and, in particular, the implementation of an environmental strategy within the VW group worldwide.

Before becoming involved in management education, he was active in German politics. He was Minister of Economics and Technology in the State of Hesse with particular responsibility for transport, traffic, and energy. Before that, he was a member of the German Bundestag, specializing in energy, technology, industry, and foreign trade issues.

John Ward – Wild Group Professor of Family Business, IMD

Professor Ward is The Wild Group Professor of Family Business at IMD, and also a professor at Northwestern University's Kellogg Graduate School of Management (USA). He is director of IMD's renowned 'Leading the Family Business' programme, in which he has taught since its inception in 1987. His teaching and research interests are in family enterprise continuity, governance, and sustainable strategy. His MBA and PhD degrees are from Stanford Graduate School of Business.

Ward has authored several books, including the bestselling *Keeping the Family Business Healthy, Creating Effective Boards for Private Enterprises,* and the just published *Strategic Planning for the Family Business*, as well as the Family Business Leadership Series (published in four languages) and numerous articles. He serves on the board of several companies in Europe and North America.

IMD

IMD is one of the world's leading business schools. Located in Lausanne, Switzerland, IMD has been helping organizations improve their performance for over fifty years. Its high standards are recognized by hundreds of the best companies around the world.

IMD was founded by a group of leading corporations to address the real challenges that international business executives face and, in the final analysis, need to win. To this day, IMD remains focused on real-world management issues – developing leadership capabilities and offering state-of-the-art concepts and tools. While other business schools primarily teach full-time graduate university students, IMD keeps an unwavering focus on the learning needs of executives and their organizations.

Executive Development from IMD

Executive Development from IMD provides cutting-edge thinking from the faculty of one of the world's leading business schools.

Each book presents concepts and insights for today's most important business and management challenges. The tone is straightforward. The message is practical. The ideas are tested and ready for managers to apply in their companies.

Each book follows a similar format: key-point summaries reinforce the message of each chapter and learning points translate concepts into action. Every chapter is illustrated with relevant international case studies that bring the discussions, analysis and recommendations to life.

Executives attend IMD programmes not only to learn but also to be inspired. The books in this series, like IMD programmes, provide executives with inspiration as well as with tools to improve themselves and make an immediate contribution to their companies. The focus is executive learning – engaging, energizing and impactful.

Preface and Acknowledgements

I n times of massive public outcry, of the type we recently observed with regard to corporate governance, it is sometimes difficult to switch from a scandal-driven to a value added-oriented approach. Corporate failure always contains important lessons, if one focuses not on moral outrage and condemnation, but rather on digging out the lessons to be learned and transforming them into an idea of how to do things better. We began this research in autumn 2000 (the pre-Enron period) under the heading of the 'Global Corporate Governance Research Initiative' and tried not to become too distracted by the volatility of the political debate.

Our main research tool was a very personal, confidential, one-on-one discussion with board members across the world (62 at the last count), in addition to the many discussions I had with participants of IMD's board programme and other programmes since 2000. Valuable input also came from the board retreats I run at IMD. To these retreats in particular I owe the insight into the relationship between corporate governance and strategy.

I know that this type of loose, unscripted, face-to-face discussion violates the rules of normal academic empirical research. But is there another way out? A chairman of a board rarely tells you why and how he had to kick out his CEO when a tape recorder is running. And I wanted to avoid the typical black box approach of academic research: take one input variable (e.g. independent directors) and measure output (e.g. financial performance), as this normally leads to inconclusive and impractical results. When one wants to shed some light into the black box, I see no other way out. My personal experience, both as a member of a managing board and numerous supervisory board assignments, certainly helped me to put unstructured information into context. But the reader should not only trust my fairness and accuracy in representing and aggregating the data – not least given my previous track record as an empirical researcher – but is also invited to test the fruitfulness of this research, especially in the two cases: War at the Helm of Elicore and National Life. These cases were written on the basis of discussions of the variety described above. They could probably have never been written as public cases.

So my thanks go to all the interviewees who devoted their time and brains to my pertinent and insistent questions, and to the participants of board retreats, who probably suffered as much from my German scepticism and punctuality as from my curiosity. But I hope that they too got something out of these discussions. Their contribution, as well as the input from various IMD participants, is especially appreciated at a time when corporate governance had become fashionable and I was most probably not the only one asking for their time.

The second source of information was the survey, where I have to praise Helga Krapf for her patience and diligence in pushing for a high response rate, and I hope that all her efforts in our research cooperation are now paying off with her PhD thesis on which she is currently working. (As this is under my supervision, I have to be careful with too much praise ...)

While the academic literature and the many (too many?) articles in journals did not so much provide new insight, as help me to benchmark my own information and frame the hypothesis that I wanted to test. Additionally, it provided me with more details about governance systems that I was until then unfamiliar with.

This book could definitely not have been written without the support of IMD.

First, our President Peter Lorange, who not only participated as a researcher in IMD's Global Corporate Governance Research Initiative (see Chapter 6: 'The Role and Responsibilities of the CEO'), but is also responsible, together with Jim Ellert, John Walsh and their teams, for the creative research culture at IMD (including the necessary budgets). Fred Neubauer, now Professor Emeritus, pushed me to gain interest in this research beyond my personal experience and helped me to set up the research project, based on his tremendous experience and insights in this area (see his article on board evaluation). Bill George and John Ward were not only valuable contributors to this book (see the case commentary by Bill George and John Ward's contribution 'How Governing Family Businesses is Different'), but helped me to understand the US system better, so that we can live up to IMD's commitment as a truly global research and learning platform. In addition

John made sure that our corporate governance research did not neglect the many other forms of incorporation aside from public quoted companies. The finance dimension of corporate governance was a useful correction to the temptation to look solely at structures of power.

In this book, authors are responsible for the content of their articles, but we made sure as a team effort that there is a 'red thread' (as outlined in the Introduction, which provides a roadmap of this book) and a common approach of 'Real World, Real Learning'.

The collaboration was a great experience, partly because all authors shared the same curiosity and knack for relevance, but also because most of us have had personal experience as board members in different countries, industries and company sizes, making for an extremely rich experience. However, while IMD's culture emphasizes teamwork, the final responsibility has to be taken by the person who spearheaded the effort. In this case it is I: a privilege that I definitely enjoyed, and a responsibility to which I hopefully live up to.

Introduction – A Roadmap for the Book

Many recent efforts of consultants and academics focus on the compliance part of corporate governance, i.e. how to keep the CEO out of jail. In contrast, our main assumption is that the major role of the board – as the company's central lever – is about leadership: setting directions, providing value added, selecting the best people and coaching them, and walking the talk. In doing so, however, every board faces several dilemmas; the why, what and how are by no means obvious – not least because the shaping influences for corporate governance differ widely and there is no one-size-fits-all approach (which today is often the implicit assumption of regulation and codes of conduct).

In Part I, 'Global Corporate Governance – Issues, Framework and Evidence for Board Leadership', Ulrich Steger introduces the basic framework and its results to shed some light into the 'black box' of corporate governance. It starts out with a critical review of the current debate to then focus, using the Swissair case as a template, on the four dilemmas the board is confronted with (often in varying, but never in irrelevant degrees): micro-management versus detachment (the division of labour and cooperation between management and board), risk taking versus financial control (the system and processes to set directions and monitor results), the eroding boundaries in global companies versus national frameworks and the conflicting expectations of stakeholders for the licence to operate.

Second, shaping factors of corporate governance – personalities, capital markets/owners, strategy and cultural/legal influences – lead to a broad variety of corporate governance systems. These are clustered into four types: CEO-dominated, checks-and-balances, owner-centred and consensus-oriented. The basic mechanisms and how they function are explained. It is argued that each of them works and is a national response to the context and needs to be met by corporate governance.

Third, the specifics of corporate governance in global companies are outlined, using DaimlerChrysler as a template. The DaimlerChrysler case is analysed to offer lessons on how such complexity can be managed.

The second part of the book deepens the analysis of three 'burning questions', touched on in Part I. Peter Lorange ('The Role and Responsibilities of the CEO') discusses in detail the relationship between the CEO and boards. Especially now that boards are more 'empowered' and stronger, each party has a responsibility to make this relationship work and complement one another in the best interest of the company.

Fred Neubauer and Helga Krapf report on framework and experiences with the evaluation of CEOs and boards. In addition to being a hot topic, evaluation is a long-standing practice in best practice boards.

In corporate governance, family business differs most from public companies (which does not mean that they cannot learn from one another). John Ward discusses these differences, specifically with regard to the different phases of the life cycle of a family business. He reviews the different roles that should be played by boards and the family in a transparent way.

In Part III, Bill George discusses three case studies, as well as providing his interpretation of the Swissair case. The first case deals with conflict in boards, focusing on the role and responsibility of the independent director. Conflict between the chairman of the board and the CEO is explored in the second case. The third case raises corporate governance issues and the stewardship responsibility of management in case of a raider attack. All three cases, plus the Swissair and DaimlerChrysler cases, were recent outputs of IMD's Global Corporate Governance Research Initiative, as was the survey that provided empirical evidence for the first part of this book.

Each of the chapters is easy to read (at least that was our intention). In addition to raising relevant issues, they also provide proven solutions to problems and ways to professionally manage the dilemmas that arise. At IMD, we meet rigorous global academic standards in our research, but we care equally about practical relevance. While the primary target group of this book are board members, company secretaries and other corporate officers, the academic world might benefit from our research, as well as the evidence and cases presented. After all, few academic institutions enjoy such a close working relationship and easy access to its research subject as IMD.

You are invited to provide your feedback on how well we measured up to our intentions by sending an email to Ulrich Steger at steger@imd.ch.

Part I

Global Corporate Governance – Issues, Framework and Evidence for Board Leadership

Ulrich Steger

1
Now that Everything is in Place, Does it Matter?

I t's a familiar pattern: a scandal erupts followed by a public outcry, and leads to a political push for new regulation – and rueful sinners search their souls and promise to better themselves.

Rarely has this pattern worked as perfectly as in the corporate governance 'reforms' of 2002. Barely known to a broader management audience, let alone the public, corporate governance rocketed to the top of the political agenda. It will take lawyers and courts years to sort out the practical relevance of the new regulation, especially in the USA, propelled through Congress by the urgent need to 'restore investors' confidence' (a noble translation for the hope to drive share prices to previous heights).

Remorseful top executives gather in blue-ribbon panels, creating 'codes of conduct', best-practice recommendations, guidelines, handbooks, etc., with a rabbit-like growth rate. Consultants and academics have not been able to resist the temptation to jump on the bandwagon: boards are probably now one of the best surveyed and researched economic institutions ever (we plead guilty here, too). And ethical advice is being dispensed by the score.

Whether mired in scandal or not, in today's interconnected world, all countries move on corporate governance in the same direction (only the 'rouge states' and notoriously corrupt countries miss out). Greece, for example, used the opportunity to try to shed its emergent market image. South Africa combined its corporate governance efforts with black empowerment. In the European Union, the commission made yet another important announcement. The list could continue nearly indefinitely. The reaction was quickest in the USA, because the most dramatic collapses happened there and created probably the provisions with the maximum bureaucratization of corporate governance. In Asia and especially Japan the response was slow, as always, but will continue (probably even when the US again switches course).

Everything is now in place: independent directors, committees of all sorts, CEOs and CFOs who are now held accountable for the figures they release (weren't they before?), auditors who should by now be watchdogs rather than lapdogs, and companies around the globe will report to which code of conduct they adhere.

Will it help placate angry shareholders and a concerned public beyond having a placebo effect? Maybe up to a point, but there are three items of bad news.

The first is that there is no evidence that any of the corporate governance structures, such as stipulations concerning the proportion of independent directors, equity ownership of management or any of the other remedies recommended (e.g. eliminate the former CEO from the board), have had any detectable impact on board performance. A revealing example is General Electric, undoubtedly one of the most successful US corporations, which in past decades had a fairly poor corporate governance structure, in light of today's standards (see Box 1.1: GE's corporate governance reforms).

Box 1.1: GE's corporate governance reforms

The corporate governance standards of General Electric (GE) under its most admired management hero, Jack Welch, are best illustrated by considering the changes his successor, Jeff Immelt, pushed through (mostly in early 2003) after GE lost approximately 50% of its market capitalization. These changes were the following:

- Strict implementation of the Sarbanes-Oxley Act[1] (e.g. Audit and Compensation Committee)
- Two-thirds of GE's directors should be independent (under a strict definition of independence[2])
- A lead director, who advises on the committee chairs and the board agenda
- Three 'executive sessions' (of independent board members) per year
- A 'strategy retreat'
- Every director should visit GE's businesses on a yearly basis, thus interacting directly with operational management
- A self-evaluation process for the GE board
- Increased responsibility for the audit committee, as well as greater financial disclosure of GE, especially its many and complex SPEs (Special Purpose Entities)

- More variable compensation, and under stricter conditions, for management and board members.

Equally important may be more on the symbolic side: GE's century-old, forbidding, dark wood-panelled boardroom was replaced by an airy meeting room with daylight.

(For details see GE's website: www.ge.com/en/commitment/governance/highlights.htm)

1 Sarbanes-Oxley Act was passed in 2002 and is also known as the public accounting reform and investor protection act. Its intention is 'To improve quality and transparency in financial reporting and independent audits and accounting services for public companies, to create a Public Company Accounting Oversight Board, to enhance the standard setting process for accounting practices, to strengthen the independence of firms that audit public companies, to increase corporate responsibility and the usefulness of corporate financial disclosure, to protect the objectivity and independence of securities analysts, to improve Securities and Exchange Commission resources and oversight, and for other purposes.' (http://www.sarbanes-oxley.com)

2 'Directors will be considered "independent" if the sales to, and buys from, GE are less than one percent of the revenues of companies they serve as executive officers, and if loans provided by GE to a company they serve as executive officers, and loans received by GE from such companies, constitute less than one percent of the total assets of such company. Moreover, if a GE director serves as an officer or director of a charitable organization, the GE director will be considered "independent," if GE donates less than one percent of that organization's annual charitable receipts.' (See GE website.)

Disney multiplied its sales and profit over two decades by nearly a factor of 20, with what a somewhat cynical observer called the 'typical' US board: the CEO, his eight friends, a woman and an African-American.

The 'black box' of corporate governance obviously defies any simple input–output relationship of the following kind: increase your number of independent directors (or any other input variable) to increase the output (in this case, financial performance). The reverse today makes more sense: Disney's CEO Michael Eisner had to relieve three friends from their board duties – a teacher, an actor and his architect – after it became obvious that the previous success factors of Disney's strategy were no longer valid. But corporate governance advocates will be hard pressed to identify and isolate any lasting impact on Disney's or GE's share price. As often, markets punish laggards, but rarely reward front-runners.

The second piece of bad news is that corporate failures will occur again. A market economy is not foolproof; on the contrary. If companies do not take risks (with a certain risk of failure), there would be no rationale for profits greater than the cost of capital. A market economy compared with other systems reveals mistakes early, forces their correction and limits the overall impact through decentralization and risk diversification. But some companies will go bankrupt due to the inability to make a sufficient response to the mistakes they unavoidably made.

All the big blunders in the past – e.g. Swissair, Vivendi, Kmart, Tyco, etc. – were due not to a lack of corporate governance structures or misapplied accounting rules, but rather a flawed strategy or a mistaken implementation. Never was a company ruined due to a failure to properly apply technical accounting rules or a lack of corporate governance structures. Rather, it was the other way around: when the strategy failed to deliver the promised and often unrealistic results, top management first began to 'massage the numbers', moving from the 'creative', to the misleading, to outright falsifying.

Enron was the most spectacular example for this pattern. First and foremost, it had a risky, verging on speculative, business model, which did not deliver on the excessively high expectations created. Somewhere along the line, Enron began cheating to cover up results delivered by the real economy.

But beyond these examples of obviously flawed business strategies (sometimes with the benefit of hindsight), it should be clear that top management and the board can err, despite having a best practice corporate governance system in place. After all, the more diffusely structured problems are, the more they tend to move up the hierarchy, eventually reaching the board. The information for the decision is often ambiguous and biased. It can be interpreted in different ways. There are a large number of influencing factors, such as unknown competitive responses and shifting macroeconomic conditions, creating complexity with little certainty of any one outcome (especially as in most cases many influencing factors – e.g. the reaction of competitors – cannot be controlled). Even the best-founded judgement can be wrong, and this cannot be prevented by any corporate governance structure (and in my view, it is even dangerous to encourage this illusory belief).

If our reasoning is correct, it has important implications for the corporate governance discussion. It shifts the focus from structure and the tendency of 'ticking boxes' to the content and context of corporate governance and its decision-making process including influencing factors, biases and the potential traps. Such an approach can add greater value for the practical work of corporate governance and its key institution, the board. However, before we go on to elaborate upon the content of corporate governance in this chapter and the rest of the book, there is a third piece of bad news.

The corporate governance discussion in public has now departed from how to best organize accountability and responsibility at the helm of the company. It has moved on to a more fundamental debate about corporate roles in society, basic attitudes and behaviours in businesses, which are perceived as more powerful than governments. Few understand the irony that 'the biggest peacetime wealth transfer in history' (Warren Buffett) occurred under the banner of shareholder value – to the detriment of shareholders and the benefit of some high-level corporate officers. Others see this already as the emerging of new class warfare. This time rather than workers versus capitalists, it is knowledge workers versus shareholders (although few CEOs fit the usual description of a knowledge worker as an expert professional with a specific know-how).

But for the broader public, the current corporate (mis-)behaviour is simply a question of greed and lack of accountability in exercise of power. 'Corporate governance is for me just the question, how can you tame the excessive greed and egregious abuse of power in the big corporations. We cannot allow spoiling the rest of society – it would blow up the whole of social fabric', stated an NGO leader voicing the opinion typical in non-business circles. Politicians – ever sensitive to shifts in public mood – do not stand on the sidelines. The result is simple: the age of deregulation is over; re-regulation is the new game in town. The Bush Administration, which can hardly be labelled anti-business, pushed more pages of regulation to the Federal Register[1] in 2002 than any other government in any given year in US history. In Europe, the shift will be slow, because new regulations have tended to overcompensate for the abolishment of old prescriptions. And media scrutiny of corporate deeds (and especially misdeeds) will not go away. Since CEOs have started competing with film divas for public attention, they are now subject to the same media rules: you are twice as long 'written down' as you have been 'written up'.

What are the main implications of this – somewhat brief – evaluation of the current corporate governance debate? As discussed, it means we need to avoid the dominant focus on structures. After all 'structure follows strategy' is one of the most fundamental wisdoms of management. First, you have to be clear about your corporate governance strategy and its leadership contribution. Just as in any other business function, how to add value remains the key imperative. This requires first and foremost examining – as in any other strategy formulation – the corporate governance context and content and clearly defining the goal to be achieved. (The current dominant goal appears to be keeping the CEO out of jail, which we consider as necessary, but merely complying with the law is insufficient. For this purpose alone, a board is probably not necessary.)

After this consideration, we look at structures and processes appropriate to achieve this goal. In particular, the processes for decision making, the method of cooperating and contributing to provide leadership require greater attention than the formal structure indicators, which dominate the current debate.

Therefore in this chapter of the book we try to adopt a value added corporate governance focus. In Chapter 2, we analyse where corporate governance failed in the strategic dimension, rather than the structural or formal dimension. We use the Swissair case as a template for this analysis, and derive the four fundamental dilemmas that each board has to confront.

Based on this consideration, in Chapter 3 we analyse the fit between the business environment (context) and the corporate governance clusters identified, and we explore and critically review one basic assumption of many codes of conduct – that there is *a* best practice of corporate governance. This is also where we discuss issues of board leadership and working processes in greater detail.

Chapter 4 deals with the specifics of corporate governance in global companies, confronted with many different rules and regulations that find themselves very much in the public spotlight due to their sheer size (DaimlerChrysler serves as an example here).

In Chapter 5 we look ahead and discuss some of the nagging questions of corporate governance.

2
How can Corporate Governance Fail?

Corporate governance and the Swissair grounding[1]

From the outside, Swissair's corporate governance structure appeared irreproachable. All members of the *Verwaltungsrat*, the body which under Swiss law has the ultimate responsibility for leading the company (*Gesamtleitungsfunktion*), included outside directors who had outstanding track records as bankers and industrialists (only one was a former senior manager). It was a 'legion of honour' (and previously based not just on prestige of the members but also on seniority; members were advised to keep quiet for the first two years).

Over the years, the government influence had waned, although some of the Swiss cantons held an important minority share (led by the Canton of Zurich, which also owns Zurich Airport). Only two of the ten board members came from the civil service – roughly in line with the shareholding. The Swiss desire for elite consensus remained strong. The board had a detailed list of duties, enshrined in the company's Articles of Association and three committees – (1) finance, which basically also functioned as an audit committee in today's language; (2) organization, including group personnel policy; and (3) remuneration. The meetings were held on a monthly basis and the long-time non-executive chairman, a retired CEO, was responsible for the board agenda and information flow.

The management was responsible for running the company. Philippe Bruggisser, who had been the COO since 1995 and CEO since 1997, had a track record for first turning around Swissair's service division and then staging the airline's return to profitability (after losses in 1995 and 1996). Together with Lukas Mühlemann (the former head of McKinsey Switzerland, who became CEO of SwissRe in 1994 and of Crédit Suisse in 1997), Bruggisser tried to tackle two strategic dilemmas for Swissair. First, there was a threat that the airline would be locked out of the emerging European aviation market, due to deregulation within the EU. Second, it was too small to be a global player in the consolidating industry and too big (and too proud) to become a second-tier feeder[2] airline in one of the big aviation alliances. An attempt to merge with other mid-sized airlines in 1993 failed due to political resistance in Switzerland. To resolve these dilemmas, an aggressive acquisition strategy (labelled the 'Hunter Strategy' by McKinsey) was undertaken. The goal was to acquire 10 to 25% stakes in a number of airlines, including Finnair, Austrian Airlines and Irish Aer Lingus, to form a European pole for an alliance with a big US carrier (at that time Delta). In addition, the services (maintenance, catering, IT) were to be expanded and sold to the group members.

However, as one board member later admitted, the Hunter Strategy was 'proving more difficult to implement than expected'. Most of the originally targeted airlines declined to join the Qualiflyer Alliance under Swissair leadership. So after taking a 49.5% stake in Sabena in 1995, Bruggisser acquired 49% of French Air Littoral and 49% of German charter carrier LTU in 1998. In 1999, Swissair acquired a 49% share in each of the following: French AOM and Air Liberté, Italian Volare Group and Air Europe. An attempt to secretly increase the stake in Austrian Airlines failed, resulting in Austrian Airlines pulling out of Qualiflyer and switching to Lufthansa's Star Alliance. A 20% stake of South African Airlines was acquired. In 2000, Polish LOT (37%) and Portuguese TAP (20%) completed the shopping spree (but TAP was never executed). However, Delta left the Qualiflyer Alliance.

2000 was already a difficult year as losses in the allied airlines exceeded CHF 700 million (after CHF 400 million in 1999). High fuel costs and restructuring costs added additional financial stress. The Hunter Strategy came under increasing criticism, but Bruggisser convinced the board to continue. He was backed by solid support from the Swiss public, who overwhelmingly wanted a strong national carrier. Rumours started to spread. There were allegations that Crédit Suisse, whose CEO and chairman Lukas Mühlemann played a leading role on the Swissair board, fired a financial analyst who had written a critical report about Swissair's financial health. The report objected to the propping up of results from gains in the pension fund (due to the booming stock market) and keeping aircraft leases off the balance sheet (declared as operational, not financial leases). In November 2000, the board continued to affirm the strategy and its confidence in the CEO. However, in January 2001, Swissair had to report a loss of CHF 2.9 billion. Bruggisser left and the Hunter Strategy was abandoned. After a transition during which the chairman of the board also took the job of CEO, the chief financial officer of Nestlé, Mario Corti, who was one of the few newer board members, took over. At the annual general meeting, seven of the ten board members resigned and the shareholders voted against legally discharging the board.

Mühlemann, one of the remaining board members, replied to the question of whether or not the board had acted with due diligence:

> The board of directors has to rely on management, which is responsible for the operational business. The board has to have a careful look at management's ideas and proposals. It has to ask critical questions and if necessary demand alternative scenarios. Our trust in management was justifiable with the record results of 1997 and 1998. Directors cannot know as much about the market, competition, customer requirements and organization of the company as a management.

The new leadership tried to break up the alliance, which proved costly (in order to reject its option to increase its stake in Sabena to 85%, Swissair had to pay CHF 430 million). The long-term auditor, who had signed off with identical statements for the previous four years and never expressed doubts or concerns, resigned in June 2001. The new auditors revised the figures for 2000, but no legal violation could be detected. Asset sales, such as the sale of Swiss Hotel & Resorts for CHF 520 million, could not really stop the bleeding. When September 11 threw the global airline industry further into decline, Swissair ran out of liquidity and grounded its fleet on 1 October, leaving 40 000 passengers stranded and sending a shockwave through a nation that prides itself on its reliability, efficiency and a 'sure eye' (symbolized in the Wilhelm Tell story). On 5 October, Mühlemann also resigned from the Swissair board.

Lessons from the Swissair case

The four board dilemmas

The big question is simply: how could this have happened? When a company fails so spectacularly, the cause cannot simply be operational inefficiencies. Nor could the root cause be detected in the corporate governance structure. Everything was in place: committees, independent directors with a track record, etc. Some critics claim that nobody on the board had in-depth experience in the aviation industry. However, this is an unconvincing argument because thousands of boards around the world have no industry experts as their members (not least because these might often be their competitors – who else knows an industry in such depth?).

In our analysis, the Swissair board failed to live up to its duties due to four dilemmas, which are typical for the work of all boards, though varying according to different contexts and relevance (however, the latter is never minor).

Dilemma 1: Micro management versus detachment

The board can easily suffocate management by being overly involved in operational details. But it can just as easily neglect its overall responsibility by being too detached, relying on limited and even biased information or, in the worst case scenario, turning a blind eye to what is going on, even when the company is going downhill or major safeguards are being violated or dubious decisions by management are going unnoticed (as happened in the frequently quoted scandals and spectacular bankruptcies, mentioned before[3]). This is independent of the legal system because even in the two-tier system, the supervisory board can unduly restrict management through excessive authorization procedures (e.g. even low investment amounts need to be approved by the supervisory board), blurring the fine line between board and management responsibility. It leads to a slow, bureaucratic decision-making and diluted responsibility. If everybody was involved and had a say, nobody can be held accountable for the results. The Soviet system perfected this organized lack of accountability; the results are well known.

Certain factors promote this type of overinvolvement: (1) the former CEO remains on the board (in the German system often as chairman of the supervisory board) and cannot let it go; (2) a weak management with bad performance; (3) following fraudulence on a larger scale; and (4) a change in ownership without a change in management, but the owner has doubts and wants to impose different goals. This is not uncommon, and occurred, for example, when private equity companies bought divisions out of conglomerates.

On the other hand, the board can be too detached. Every board has to deal with a broad range of legal compliance issues, especially in highly regulated industries (e.g. banking or insurance). A skilful management can take up all the time of the board meeting compliance issues (and due to the prescriptive nature of regulation, the board often just serves as high-ranking internal auditors). This is not to say that ensuring compliance is unimportant, but it cannot be the dominant task of the board. Another way in which the board can become detached is to involve it in minor details, but exclude it from major decisions (and there are boards that willingly comply with such an agenda). One of Parkinson's famous laws formulated this: 'In any group of decision makers, the time spent on an issue is inversely proportional to its importance.' He describes how a board nodded through the big investment plan, but was divided by a heated debate about the allocation mechanisms for the corporate parking slot.

The Swissair board showed a bias toward detachment up to the point of crisis – but with 'isles of overinvolvement'. (See the interview with Bill George in this chapter.) A few board members, notably Lukas Mühlemann, were clearly overinvolved in the formulation of the Hunter Strategy and defended it to the end. Otherwise the board really did not notice the many 'red flags', visible not only in hindsight (e.g. when has a board not noticed that management has propped up results using stock market gains from the pension fund?). It relied totally on the charismatic, strong-willed CEO (and was totally unprepared for any succession when they kicked him out) and did nothing to ensure internal checks and balances, for example through a strong CFO.

It is difficult to measure in a statistically representative manner, but based on anecdotal evidence we can assume that most companies that failed spectacularly had a similar combination of a charismatic CEO (often assuming also the role of the chairman of the board in the US) and a detached board like Swissair (but often with best practice structures). Whether you look at ABB, most of the telecoms and media companies or excessive M&A-driven growth such as in Tyco, Monsanto or Credit Suisse, this pattern is visible. Obviously nobody on the board asked some pertinent questions when an imperial CEO was driving through his vision. Even for very senior executives it is sometimes difficult to differentiate between a vision and an hallucination.

To strike the right balance requires a shared and transparent understanding of the division of labour between management and board (for more details of the board–CEO relationship, see Chapter 6 by Peter Lorange). As we will argue in detail later, there is no one-size-fits-all definition of the roles and responsibilities in corporate governance. Rather, it has to be worked out according to the specific case. Second and equally as important is the question of attitudes and behaviours. If management sees the board as intruding on its turf, as bothersome inspectors without value added, or if board members think they can run the company better than management, it will never work, regardless of what is laid down in the chapters of association, the board procedures, etc.

(See case study 'War at the Helm of Elicore' in Chapter 9.)

Dilemma 2: Risk-taking versus tight financial control

Whereas the first dilemma between detachment and micro management is very much about the division of labour and cooperation between the board and management, the second dilemma is very much about the system, and processes which the board imposes on the company to fulfil its responsibility (and ensure that they are observed by setting an example through its behaviour and leadership and by supporting an appropriate culture). Most importantly it covers the strategy development and the board's monitoring of the implementation via the controlling function. Second, it covers the internal and external auditing function to ensure compliance (we deliberately put the priorities in this order, since compliance is necessary, but by no means sufficient to become a successful company).

One, if not the only, decisive question for the value added of the board work is its contribution to strategy formulation and its effective implementation (because the vast majority of underperforming or failing companies did mess up the strategy implementation). Given today's complexity and the dynamics of global markets, the board will be hard pressed to come up with its own detailed strategy, especially in far-flung empires with many divisions. But it can ensure three things:

(1) The consistency of corporate values (often expressed in vision and mission statements), the basic business model (key and compatible requirements to earn money in an industry) and strategy content;
(2) The effectiveness of the process of strategy design and adjustment, the system by which the implementation is monitored and the organizational design to support strategy implementation; and
(3) Transparency regarding the risks involved and definition of thresholds for the acceptability of risks.

Again, the board has to strike a balance here. The more turbulent and dynamic the markets, the greater the need to instil a bias for action, while also controlling the risk and not losing sight of the strategic direction in the tactical day-to-day operations. Processes and systems can ensure (to a certain degree) a predictable outcome and due diligence in the actions. But they can also easily drown any action in a sea of bureaucratic requirements, resulting in a long list of missed opportunities.

How can a board achieve this?

To address the consistency of values, business model and strategy content, a strategy retreat of the board is helpful. Because the majority of (non-executive) board members are outsiders, they can help the top management, which tends to focus excessively on the daily business, to see the big picture and look at the fundamentals of their business. On this level, the board can raise questions from the diversity of experiences and different perspectives of its members and evaluate the competences needed. However, a deep under-standing of the industry and the corporation is needed to go beyond intuitive questions to the really tough questions. While this sounds simple, if man-agement protects itself with a barrage of experts (consultants, investment bankers) and creates a climate in which tough questions are an indication that 'you didn't get it', any critical review of strategic management initiatives will be aborted. This climate prevailed predominantly in the dot.com and telecom boom, where amazingly oversized acquisitions were nodded through boards, despite the fact that any back-of-the-envelope calculation showed the economic nonsense of such deals. This leads to the question of whether it is the duty of boards to calm down the hype, for example, created by sales pitches of investment bankers. (My personal answer is yes.)

With regard to the second question – the process design – board members generally know through their own experience what works under certain conditions and what does not. Being clear about the process enables the board to duplicate the results of the strategy considerations, to understand the basic assumptions and the plausibility of the conclusions. They can also verify whether the organization (structure, processes, but also incentives) is supportive of strategy implementation. But what is crucial is the *permanent* monitoring of financial and non-financial results. This is not a trivial task because it requires the ability to differentiate between the random volatility of market dynamics and a more fundamental deviation from the strategic track, where numbers appear at first not to be different from the normal volatility. Looking at the corporate governance disasters, the boards omitted this task in particular, and let things slide in the wrong direction for too long. The amount of data that is generated today by IT-backed controlling systems is more often than not an obstacle due to the sheer amounts of information, which is deterring. A board is well advised not to let itself be overwhelmed by what is technically possible, but instead to define clearly its own need for information: more lead indicators, benchmarks to discover deviation, relationships of members beyond raw data input. The details greatly depend on the company's specific situation.

The third task is then to look at the risk involved in any strategy, how to manage it through appropriate risk management systems and to define the accepted level of risk, as is done today with greater sophistication in the financial services industry. But every manufacturing company can build on such experiences, since in methodological terms it does not matter whether you are looking at risks associated with currency trading or a new market entry in a developing country.

If the board has done its job in strategy design and implementation, the compliance part is much easier, since any reports from internal or external auditors then fit neatly into an interpretive framework, making it much easier to understand issues (or alert the board if the watch-dogs don't address issues that had arisen in controlling or risk management).

The Swissair board also failed to address this dilemma properly. Although it was obvious that the Hunter Strategy did not work out as planned (the desired airline targets could not be hunted), the board did not instigate a correction of the strategy or even a critical review.

As one example: the experience with Sabena could have taught Swissair how much money, management resources and time it would take to bring a low-quality airline with militant unions back to profitability (hopefully). Nevertheless, in France and Italy airlines (or stakes in them) were acquired, which exceeded all the negative characteristics of Sabena. Obviously top management did not really use the board as a sounding board nor did the board express its doubts. Swissair behaviour was reminiscent of the old boy scout joke: 'after we lost all orientation, we doubled our efforts'. If management does not learn from difficulties in the course of the strategy implementation, clearly the board needs to step in and ensure that new experiences and facts are not ignored. The Swissair board did not question the smoke and mirror attempt by management to disguise the deteriorating financial results of the Hunter Strategy (e.g. to offload the airplanes from the balance sheet by declaring them operational leases, which later had to be corrected). And last but not least, many did not understand the risks of the Hunter Strategy, and yet they did not push for an appropriate risk management system with a defined level of acceptable risk. According to empirical evidence, such a gap is not uncommon on today's boards. This vacuum allows a management with the attitude 'right or wrong – my strategy' to bet the company.

The difficulty of assessing risks in joint ventures or minority stakes in companies in other countries has grown in importance due to globalization into a new dimension. We therefore consider this as the third fundamental board dilemma.

Dilemma 3: Eroding boundaries in global companies versus national legal and cultural frameworks

In the good old days, in the Frankfurt suburb of Hoechst, you could walk around a several kilometre-long red brick wall of the *Farbwerke Hoechst*, one of the three big integrated chemical companies in Germany. While there were subsidiaries, they were more like cloned parts of the mother company, designed by a 1500-person strong engineering department, manned by the corporate HR department and working according to plans from the corporate strategy planning department. Not any more. Any CEO of a globally active company probably does not know where his empire begins and where it ends. Like the Spanish Emperor Charles V, he or she can say: 'in my empire, the sun never goes down'. One finds fully owned or majority-owned subsidiaries, joint ventures with varying degrees of involvement and stakes, strategic alliances with or without underlying share swaps, consortia for a wide range of projects, on- and offshore special-purpose entities (which came into the public spotlight through Enron) and special holdings companies (for tax reasons) in easily more countries than the board can ever visit. This boundary erosion is typical of globalization and creates an ambiguity and complexity in today's world, which is fundamentally different from the past.

Box 2.1: Central characteristics of globalization
In approaching the phenomenon of globalization, one must first ask: what is specifically new about it? In what way does it break with the

previous trend of development? Globalization is understood here as a new kind of change – a 'changed change', affecting not only economic structures, but also the entire social and institutional make-up of our society. The phenomena concerned can be subsumed analytically under six central characteristics of globalization:

1. Boundary erosion

As a central feature of globalization, boundary erosion refers to the blurring of existing boundaries, the increasing permeability or even the dissolution of frontiers. This development affects not only state frontiers, but also boundaries within society and between economic units and cultures. Many problems connected with globalization are decisively influenced by the fact that boundary erosion is proceeding at very different speeds in different spheres.

The dissolution of boundaries is least advanced in politics and between states, especially as developments here are very contradictory. For example, although cross-frontier policies are now more frequent as a result of agreements, international treaties, and arrangements between states, the immigration policies of many nation states are more restrictive now than in the late nineteenth century.

By contrast, boundaries within society and cultures are disintegrating more rapidly. The biographies of people today evolve in conjunction with very diverse religious, social and cultural influences. Cultural boundary erosion thus has far-reaching effects on the identities of individuals.

Boundary erosion is undoubtedly most advanced in the economic sphere. It is seen in the liberalization and expansion of worldwide availability of information and the splitting of the commercial value-creation chain into activities distributed throughout the world.

One of the motors of boundary erosion is technical progress. The development of the communications industry has meant that the effects of individual actions extend much further than before. The cause–effect chains of social, political and economic actions are therefore extended at the same time; an overview of the world is made more difficult.

2. Heterarchy

Heterarchy refers to the transformation of hierarchical structures, characterized by clear relationships of dominance and subordination, into cooperative organizational forms, marked by reciprocal and asymmetrical dependency.

3. Transformation of structures

It is hardly possible for any actor today to attain his goals without the support of, or coordination with, other actors. In frequently self-organizing networks, individuals and institutions have a higher degree of autonomy and a greater number of behaviour options. At the same time, the newly created structures are more flexible and therefore less stable.

4. Factor mobility

A direct consequence of boundary erosion is the *high and increasing mobility*, not only of raw materials, goods and services, but also of capital and knowledge as factors of production. This factor mobility heightens competitive pressures and thus promotes market efficiency. However, the worldwide integration of the markets for capital and labour, for example, has advanced to very different degrees. This difference contributes to the problems resulting from globalization: states compete for the elusive production factor: capital. As a result, the position of the far less mobile factor – labour – and, above all, the position of groups excluded from the labour process, is deteriorating.

5. Legitimacy erosion

In the age of globalization, responsibilities often cannot be allocated clearly. This results both from increasing boundary erosion and from the form in which heterarchy is organized. This phenomenon, referred to as legitimacy *erosion*, can be detected at all levels of society: the weakened role of nation states reduces the general acceptance of laws and regulations, corporations are both hunters and hunted in the global competition, and the same individuals in their different roles are often both 'agents' and 'victims' of globalization.

6. Past–future asymmetry

Under the heading of *past–future asymmetry*, it is observed that the future can no longer be regarded as a linear continuation of the past. In highly complex, dynamic interaction systems, change takes place discontinuously, while developments are becoming less predictable in all areas of society. Connections unrecognized yesterday can become dominant influences today, and ruptures may occur unexpectedly, even in trends that have been stable for many years.

7. Variety of options

One consequence of the numerous changes, and especially of past–future asymmetry, is the variety of options open to both institutions and individuals. The spectrum of possible futures prompts a diverse range of responses. But with the gain in choice comes the pain of indecision: fields of action are increasingly marked by ambivalence and ambiguity, so that flexible behaviour and variable reactions to the continuously changing context of decision making are called for. The disappearance of all certainties gives rise to individual anxieties and collective extremisms: even more so as opportunities and risks are unevenly distributed in a global, boundary-eroded society. For highly qualified people there is a much higher probability that the diverse opportunities will work to their advantage than for unqualified people.

For the board this poses a new dilemma, because they still work in national legal and cultural contexts. The country of incorporation requires that companies meet the legal obligations of different approaches to incorporation. In Europe this is often a legal person with organs versus the US approach of an association of stockholders. Also, there are often contradicting specific requirements. For example, in the US, the CEO and CFO now have to personally certify the accounts, whereas in the European context it is the legal obligation of the full board. Also, Germany and some other European countries require employee representation on the board, but employees are not counted as 'independent', such that a German supervisory board can never have a majority of independent directors. The more specific corporate governance law has recently become, the more frequently these provisions clash (see Chapter 4).

But beyond the trickier legal compliance, the more fundamental dimension is economic. Swissair was not the only example where a cash drain of unknown or underestimated risk in foreign countries brought a company nearly to its knees. Just think of Gerling Insurance (its US reinsurance business), ABB (US-asbestos liabilities) or Texas Utility TXU (losses in Europe's deregulated markets) as recent examples. If you don't lose cash, you might lose your reputation (and the CEO and chairman might lose their jobs) as with Dutch retailer Ahold, when massive cooking of the books was discovered in the US.

In all cases, the question is raised: why didn't the board properly assess the risk and ensure protective measures?

With a more benign attitude one might ask the question: could the board see the risks ahead of time or are such failures the price of global operation? Certain risks are obviously not on the radar screen of certain cultures: the ruthlessness of US lawyers, that a whole local management team would cheat in collusion, the possibility of contracts not being legally enforceable, etc. The answer is never black and white. Whereas in the Swissair case it could be argued that the board could have made a more detailed and sober review of the detectable risks (and eventually led to consequences for the acquisitions), the ABB board in the early 1990s could probably not have sensed that the asbestos liability would exceed the provisions made during the due diligence process by more than an order of magnitude (and also hit ABB at a time when it was highly vulnerable).

Dilemma 4: Drive for shareholder value in global markets versus societal expectations of the corporate licence to operate

Big companies are regarded as public institutions. Despite the rhetoric about the footloose enterprise in a global world, if it invests physical assets, a company has many links to its business environment. The nature of the relationship varies according to the issues, the stage of economic development, the culture and political system. Globalization and deregulation have weakened certain links, often the direct, heavy-handed approach, but not the informal, indirect influences. Examples abound: in South Africa, pharmaceutical companies voluntarily agreed to deliver AIDS medicine for much lower prices than in developed countries; in Korea, the car industry agreed to limit its worker lay-offs; in Germany, industry voluntarily agreed to reduce greenhouse gas emissions. Even the incarnation of global entrepreneurship is not free of the emotional links to its home country: GE donated $20 million to the victims of September 11, but not for the victims of the civil war in Congo. In all of these situations, the companies had good reason to behave as they did – because of the risk of more severe consequences or damage to an image or brand.

At the same time, global capital markets press for ever-increasing returns and do not tolerate actions without a defined business focus. Share prices of pharmaceutical companies declined when the companies 'gave in' to the pressure in South Africa and reduced prices of drugs to treat HIV. Not firing people for overall employment reasons would probably damage the share price of a company twice as much as it gained from laying off workers.

Companies have to balance these demands and it is the board that finally decides where to strike the balance.

In the Swissair case the question is, did the board strike the right balance? There was never any open debate with regard to whether a small country like Switzerland (7.3 million inhabitants) needed an international airline and, if so, who should shoulder the price tag in case it could not do so under competitive conditions. In 1993, after its failed attempt to merge with Scandinavian Airlines, Austrian Airlines and Dutch KLM, one member of the Swiss government noted: 'Replacing the Wilhelm Tell (the medieval Swiss freedom hero) statue with a statue of the Dalai Lama would give rise to the same political feelings as if Swissair merged with a foreign airline.' That Swissair should stay independent became an unquestioned basic assumption in its strategy, culminating in the Hunter Strategy, which turned out to be a clear overstretch.

While in other cases such crucial political assumptions did not shape the strategy as with Swissair, it is far from being the only example. Monsanto gambled that the US government would ensure market access in Europe for genetically modified organisms, as did Chiquita with bananas (both were wrong). ABB would not have invested so heavily in Eastern Europe and Russia without the encouragement of the Swedish Government – just to name some recent examples.

But even when politics exerts only a small influence, it is a constraint the board has to deal with and at least create transparency about the options – and the costs and benefits in commercial terms.

Corporate governance and the Swissair grounding: an interview with Bill George

Q: What surprised you most when you read the Swissair case?

A: There were a number of surprises, but the greatest one was that the failure of Swissair's corporate strategy remained unchallenged and even unnoticed for so long. The strategy was flawed and the board had a clear responsibility for that. While Bruggisser was not blameless, one really needs to look to the board for its failure in strategy. This failure is multi-faceted and appears in a number of ways: (1) in the financial risk the corporation took; (2) the fact that it acquired only minority positions in other firms which didn't provide it with any real leverage over these firms; (3) its acquisition of very weak airlines; and (4) its expansion beyond the airline business. The board put the company in a position where it was vulnerable to bankruptcy. When September 11 happened, it was in a bad situation. It was obvious that the airline was in deep trouble before that.

Q: So the board was not sufficiently involved in determining Swissair's strategy?

A: It was a mixture of overinvolvement and negligence. On the one hand, the Swissair board was very involved in strategy – perhaps overly so. For example, Lukas Mühlemann was the head of the McKinsey office in Zurich, one of the most powerful McKinsey offices in the world. He proposed a strategy to Swissair in 1994, centering on broadening out and acquiring other airlines. In May 1995, Mühlemann joined the board. This appears to be a clear conflict of interest.

On the other hand, the board did not follow up on how the strategy worked, and it was detached from what was going on. Maybe a few board members saw the writing on the wall, but kept silent. This is a big argument in corporate governance: to what extent should boards be involved in strategy? The general consensus is that only the management has a detailed enough understanding of the business to develop a strategy that can be executed within the firm. It is the board's role to review and approve the strategic options and then to ultimately decide, which the Swissair board did, and then to oversee implementation, which obviously did not happen.

Q: But the world is hoping that independent directors on boards will prevent corporate disasters. All of the Swissair *Verwaltungsrat* were – in a legal sense – independent...

A: What does it mean to be independent? Here we have people who are linked beyond pure financial needs: they were on each other's boards and knew one another. It was the Club of Zurich, the elite of Swiss industry. But it didn't raise any critical questions. There were too many linkages for members to turn against one another in the boardroom. They were not very independent, and this resulted in a great tragedy.

Q: And what did this mean for the working of the board?

A: In the case, Benedict Hentsch made a comment: 'The Swissair board was like a legion of honour.' And as a result, he didn't ask many questions in his first two years, because he felt too young. The day you set foot in the boardroom, you are responsible for the corporation. When the majority of the board resigned in early 2001, perhaps that is what they were doing. Or perhaps they were getting out.

Mühlemann stated that the 'board of directors has to rely on management'. This statement is a defence, since it's clear that Mühlemann was doing more than that. He was intimately involved with the strategy and served on the board. Before Swissair went bankrupt, it only had three board members left. Perhaps these board members were overly concerned about their public images.

Q: Is there another area where this working style of the board led to the unchecked development of strategic problems?

A: The acquisition strategy itself was such an example. Companies are much easier to run when you control 100% of the businesses. When you control 49.5% of Sabena, 37.6% of LOT and 20% of South African Airlines, those investments are more complicated than they're worth. You can never get the efficiencies that you would get having 100% ownership. In addition, the board did not consider the political realities of taking these additional airlines on. Everyone knew that Sabena was a very poor airline, was always in financial difficulty, and the only reason that it survived was because it received funding from the Belgian government. To take on that burden of an airline that was rife with union problems between French- and Flemish-speaking unions, strikes me as a very questionable decision. You don't have the flexibility to lay off people. Switzerland has not had a strike since 1936. Labour relations are critical for the airline business. It was very poor judgement on the board's part.

3
Shedding Some Light into the Black Box

As mentioned in Chapter 1, many empirical investigations try to establish an input–output relationship, using corporate governance as a black box. Our approach was different. We tried first to see the bigger picture and asked: 'What are the shaping factors of globalization and to which types or clusters do they lead?' In addition, we tried to find patterns of working mechanisms.

Forces that shape corporate governance beyond legal frameworks

Regardless of whether companies were, for example, based in an Anglo-Saxon legal context, or in a traditional 'Rhine-Model',[1] they saw the need to develop their corporate governance in a way that fitted the global marketplace. The shaping forces are located both internally as well as externally to a company: personalities, business model and strategy, capital market and the rules and laws (see Figure 3.1).

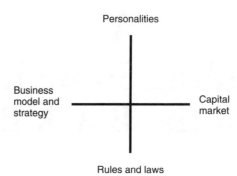

Figure 3.1 The four determinants of corporate governance practice

Probably most important is the *business model and strategy* a company pursues. Corporate governance for a bold strategy of growth in rapidly changing, volatile markets requires a different practice from more cautious development in a more mature market, due to different levels of risk taking, variances in speed and responsiveness required, etc. Indeed, we observed that with a fundamental shift in strategy, the corporate governance practice also changed.

Capital market expectations shift rapidly (not only between boom and bust and not always with any apparent logic). It is because of investment banks that companies nowadays report more according to sectors or business units, thereby making it more difficult to hide unprofitable company parts. In general, capital market expectations come in waves: demands for greater transparency are followed by calls for more independent directors, then by the need for committees (especially for audit purposes). The next wave will most likely be the need for empirical evidence of the influence that such measures exert on company performance.

The broader set of *rules and laws* in various countries (the often unwritten dos and don'ts) also has a bearing on corporate governance. Direct corporate governance laws have surprisingly little influence on the functioning of boards (i.e. these laws mostly apply when something goes wrong). In addition to the two most common types of boards (unitary and two tier), our research revealed various other board structures. We saw unitary boards where an independent chairman and the majority of outside directors supervised the executive board members, much like the two-tier boards under German law. Analogously, we also found in the German system configurations where the CEO limits his communication to only a bit more than the direct report to the chairman of the supervisory board. Issues such as how to network (open and fluid versus close-knit old boy networks) and the obligations towards society are further areas of the written and unwritten rules, which shape corporate governance in a certain cultural and political framework.

Last, but not least, are the *personalities* involved. Towering people with excellent track records and powerful connections will always be central to decision making, regardless of how the process is defined. Since the 1998 merger between Daimler and Chrysler, DaimlerChrysler has had three distinctive formal governance systems (see Chapter 4). But irrespective of the form of organization, nobody doubts that CEO Jürgen Schrempp was always firmly in control.

However, beyond the influence of the stars of a corporation, personal chemistry between board members, top executives and the chairman is also of great importance. Problems are often blurry, questions and potential outcomes not clearly defined. The basis for decision making is therefore uncertain, and forecasts are difficult. Some might argue that this is not a new phenomenon when it comes to decisions in top management. However, in uncertain conditions in particular, variables like trust, competence, personal character and integrity become more important. If the chemistry at the top of the organization is not right, then the best systems will prove useless. And true visionaries will be able to implement their strategies regardless of the system in place (although only the future will tell whether this idea is a good one for business). (For more details of the relationship between CEOs and boards see Chapter 6 by Peter Lorange.)

The result: Four distinct corporate governance clusters

From these four determinants one can derive and observe four clusters of typical corporate governance models, which focus on how companies organize their corporate governance practices and systems (rather than the ostensible legal system).

In the *CEO-centred* model, one person is clearly in charge and leads the company. This model is frequently found in the US, where the role of CEO is still often combined with that of the chairman of the board. It is also found in France, where the president/*directeur-général* plays a dominant role regardless of whether the company opts for a unitary board structure (with a single administrative board *conseil d'administration*) or a two-tier structure (with executive committee *directoire* and supervisory board *conseil de surveillance*). It allows for quick decisions, but tends to be a system with few checks and balances: not many CEOs allow a strong board that can challenge, or even stop, him or her controlling the risk associated with often bold actions.

This structure often develops when a CEO has been long serving at the company and has a good track record and especially if all potential rivals have left the company. Of course, rapid decision making is only an advantage if the quality of decisions is high and if risks continue to be calculated. However, succession is always a problem in these companies, because, as one chairman of the board put it, 'It's difficult for new things to grow in the shadow of a big tree.'

In the *checks-and-balances* model, there is a clear division between executive and supervisory roles. It is found not only in Germany in two-tier boards (i.e. executive and supervisory) but also in the UK, where the non-executive chairman and the majority of the independent directors define the boundaries within which the CEO and top management team can operate. For example, at BP in 2002 the unitary board had 11 non-executive and four executive members. Here the non-executive directors are also often in charge of evaluating the CEO (and management board) systematically and periodically, as well as initiating the succession of a CEO.

However, implementing a true balance of power is difficult. There is often a shift of power, especially if a major change occurs in the company's strategy. There's also evidence that the centre of power shifts from 'control' to 'execution' as companies grow in size, globalize and gain in organizational complexity. In such situations boards often try to regain some form of control by regularly evaluating the CEO and executive management. In this way, succession and executive selection processes gain importance in the work of boards and corporate governance.

In the *owner-centred* model, a big shareholder (or in privately held companies the family) pulls the strings on important issues. Their involvement in day-to-day business can vary, as can the mechanisms they employ. Equity funds, which aim to guide underperforming companies back to performance in order to make them attractive for future buyers, work with financial control mechanisms. In these companies, corporate governance systems are only of secondary interest since important duties, such as succession planning, strategy decisions or risk management, are carried out by the fund. Long-term owners often successfully ensure the representation of their interests through culture: management works in their interest (rather than in the interest of minority shareholders). The US investor-guru Warren Buffett and the Quandt family at BMW are famous for having instilled in managers the need to have uppermost in their minds the question: 'What does our owner think?' The Ford family always steps in when things get tough. Others, such as the tycoon-turned-prime-minister Silvio Berlusconi, are known for occasionally becoming embroiled in even small business details.

The *consensus-oriented* model looks at long-term relationships of the board with non-executive owners and also other stakeholders of a company, such as banks, suppliers and customers. While closer relationships facilitate access to funding and the possibility of a longer-term view, this model is slow when it comes to decision making. Additionally, the relationships are often built on a system of cross-shareholdings, a situation that international investors in Germany and Japan, for example, have long criticized for lack of transparency. It is also typical in the segments of society dominated by old boy networks, including the business environment. This is typical in emerging markets where relationships of trust remain more important than the newly evolving capitalist institutions, sometimes reinforced by societal expectations (for example, in Asia, inviting important stakeholders onto the board).

Asked in our survey to categorize their company in one of the four clusters, more than half of the respondents chose checks and balances. However, when asked for the organization of their corporate governance, many more companies reported a separation of control and execution. Table 3.1 presents a summary of the survey results.

A total reconciliation of approach and system (i.e. separate chairman and CEO would translate into checks and balances or consensus-oriented approaches, but not separation into CEO dominated) would come close to being a miracle. Such clusters are never stable (see below). The corporate governance of every company needs its own analysis, but the clusters can help to categorize specific, but basically similar situations.

In this regard, it is more interesting to look at how companies with a certain legal corporate governance framework (i.e. one- versus two-tier systems) perceive their corporate governance work in practice. Table 3.2 represents

Table 3.1 Survey results: perceived and practised corporate governance

Perceived corporate governance approach	Practised corporate governance system
54% Checks and balances	76% Separate chairman and CEO
26% CEO dominated	15% No separate chairman/CEO function
7% Consensus oriented	2% Lead director and CEO
7% Owner dominated	7% Other
6% Other	

Source: For more detailed results please see the IMD working paper by Steger, U. and H. Krapf (2003): 'Corporate Governance in Global Companies – Content not Structure as the Main Driver'.

Table 3.2 Corporate governance approach versus system spread over systems

	CEO centred	Checks and balances	Consensus oriented	Owner dominated	Other	Total
Separate CEO and chairman	40	99	13	12	10	174
	22.99%	56.90%	7.47%	6.90%	5.75%	100%
No separate function	11	16	2	2	2	33
	33.33%	48.48%	6.06%	6.06%	6.06%	100%
Lead director and CEO	3	1	0	1	0	5
	60%	20%		20%		100%
Other	6	8	0	1	1	16
	37.50%	50%		6.25%	6.25%	100%
Total	60	124	15	16	13	228
	26.32%	54.80%	6.58%	7.02%	5.70%	100%

a cross-tabulation of approach versus system, over both the approach and the system.

Looking at the breakdown of the corporate governance system practised over the perceived corporate governance approach, it's obvious that even in companies with a separate CEO and chairman function, CEOs dominate the company's corporate governance practice in a perceived 23% of companies. At the other extreme, even when there is no separation between CEO and chairman, and one would assume a CEO-centred system, nearly half the respondents considered themselves in the checks-and-balances cluster.

The first result proves again the influence of the four forces. If the personalities are such that a CEO is a strong personality, then he dominates the corporate governance system regardless of formally established control and balance mechanisms.

However, we ask our readers to take the statistics with even more than a grain of salt. The responses are probably biased by political correctness considerations (or 'sugar-coated' as the Chinese used to say). These days, one does not easily admit that the company is run as a one-man show. The interviews and other qualitative indicators (including my own board experience), however, suggest that variations of the consensus-oriented model are predominant in the board reality.

First, as we have outlined above, a true 'checks-and-balances' model is difficult to maintain, due to factors ranging from the institutional framework to personalities. Every tension at the very top of the company might ripple down to become an earthquake, increasing politics and distracting senior managers from the focus of the business. In addition, for an individual board member, the incentives to conform are considerable. One can't raise one's voice on every issue since board meeting schedules are usually overfull and time to discuss issues is limited. There is also a natural mismatch between the huge apparatus of the company and the comparatively small board. How can an individual board member question carefully formulated strategy papers developed by the strategy department and external consultants? The potential personal results of such confrontations are uncertain: in a best case scenario the board member will be regarded as maverick; in the worst case he or she will be eliminated from the board.

We would also like to emphasize the importance of perception in this connection. Out of the 12 replies from the US, seven reported a combined CEO and chairman function. The same companies also perceived their system to be one of checks and balances. However, this is an outside point of view; many board members certainly perceive it in this way. We have to accept that their perception is the reality as they see it; however, they do not always act accordingly. But the bottom line is that today the majority accepts in principle that even at the helm of hierarchical organizations like corporations, power should not go unchecked.

Are these corporate governance models stable over time?

Each model is a self-contained corporate governance system, with distinctive strengths as well as weaknesses. For example, the checks-and-balances model is most effective in CEO selection and control, but often lacks strategic input. In the CEO-centred model, it is the other way around, with quick decision making and strategy implementation promoted. The suitability of one of these four models to a particular company at a particular stage in the company life cycle and in a particular business environment may therefore change over time. A company may change the model if the business situation requires. In once instance, a company changed from a checks-and-balances model (with a separate chairman and CEO, and an executive and a supervisory board) to a CEO-centred model with a unitary structure when it started to pursue an ambitious M&A (mergers and acquisitions) growth strategy in a consolidating industry. The need for quick decision making and swift implementation and monitoring of the chosen strategy was better met by the new system with the former CEO now called 'executive chairman'. The chairman's office was responsible for strategy and

M&A, whereas the successor, called 'managing director', was responsible for operation only.

Overall, 63% of participating companies had experienced a shift in their corporate governance approach in the last three to five years. Figure 3.2 shows a breakdown per region. Quite surprisingly, nearly two-thirds of Anglo-Saxon companies reported a change compared to 'just' 55% of companies in Northern Europe. When thinking about the perceived gap between European and Anglo-Saxon corporate governance, one would have expected longer-lasting corporate governance traditions in Anglo-Saxon countries and hence a lower change rate than in the other regions. Companies named different triggers for these changes in corporate governance approaches:

Own board discussion	48.6%
Voluntary code of conduct	46.6%
Changes in law	31.5%
Shareholder pressure	20.5%
Other	16.4%
Mergers and acquisitions	5.5%

While 37% of respondents did not report any changes in corporate governance at all, among those that reported changes in their corporate governance approach, board discussions were one of the most frequently named reasons for such changes. On the one hand, boards live in the real world and are more influenced by media, political discussions, and moves by their peers and competitors, so the response is plausible. On the other hand, it signalled greater proactivity than what we have seen in reality.

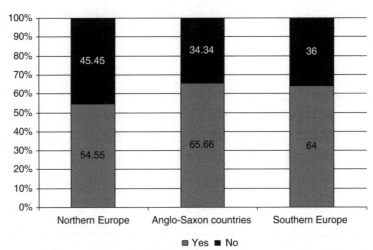

Figure 3.2 Have you observed a shift in your corporate governance approach in the last 3–5 years?

However, boards can only actively and successfully involve themselves in such decisions if they actively engage in setting the company's strategy. As Bill George, former Medtronic chairman and CEO, put it: 'Rather than focusing on short-term stock prices, boards should be asking questions like: Are we being true to our mission and our values? Are we building shareholder value for the long term? How are we sustaining our growth? What risks are we taking to get there?' If such questions are thoroughly thought through and honestly answered, a board should be able to recognize the need and strategic value of a change to another corporate governance model.

How involved are boards in practice?

Besides the legal and the strategic aspects of the board's duties, board members should also be engaged in the selection and evaluation of the top executive team, and especially the CEO. Specialized board committees have become increasingly popular in recent years to promote these tasks. More generally, the meeting frequency and the total time spent carrying out their duties are indicators of how involved board members are. Succession planning ensures continuity of the work. In addition, committees and regular evaluations are regarded as means of controlling executive management by boards. Finally, getting involved with the external business environment becomes more and more part of the role of boards.

Board committees

We asked company secretaries if their companies had audit, nomination, personnel/reward, sustainability or other committees. According to our research, three-quarters of companies had an audit committee in place. In 97% of cases this audit committee was chaired by an independent director and not an executive, regardless of the corporate governance system in place. Strategy committees, in contrast, were rare. Only 32 out of 232 companies had such a committee, and the majority (17) were chaired by an inside executive. One can conclude that in the other cases, strategy was simply not considered a topic for a committee or that the board of directors did not systematically deal with strategy. Figure 3.3 shows an overall breakdown of the results.

When we break down this result for different regions, we see more trends. Anglo-Saxon companies clearly favour independent directors, except with regard to strategy committees. Here only 23% of committees (as opposed to 58% in Northern European companies) were reported as chaired by an independent director. Although we did not receive enough replies for a statistically significant result for Southern European countries, there is still

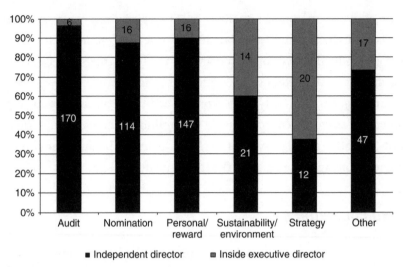

Figure 3.3   Overall breakdown of board committees

a visible trend: inside executive directors are more frequently chairmen of committees than in the other two regions.

Board organization and working processes

The effectiveness of boards depends on different factors: one is their size. The bigger a group the more difficult discussions and decision making become. The global average of boards in our study was 12 members. However, the range in the number of board members is large, even within the different regions. The largest average boards can be found in Germany (15.7 members), France (15.7) and Spain (15.2), while the smallest boards are in Switzerland (8.6), Australia (8.5) and Finland (7.2). Boards need to find a balance between having enough diversity in the group while still being able to work efficiently.

The overall average of hours spent in board meetings per annum is 22 hours. However, boards meet more frequently in Anglo-Saxon countries than in Northern European countries. Whereas the majority (54%) of Anglo-Saxon boards meet on a monthly basis, 47% of Northern European boards meet quarterly. Surprisingly, despite the difference in frequency, most board meetings last for four hours in both regions. Shorter or longer meetings show nearly the same distribution. Chairman and CEOs meet more frequently. In Anglo-Saxon countries the majority (47%) meets weekly, whereas in Northern European countries the majority (33%) meets on a monthly basis.

In companies with a separate CEO and chairman, the tasks of calling supervisory board meetings and agenda preparation are equally shared between the two in 32% of the cases overall. However, in Northern European countries the chairman is more likely to call meetings whereas in Anglo-Saxon countries, the CEO tends to perform this duty. However, strategy proposals are mostly made by the CEO: 73% globally, and 79% for both Anglo-Saxon as well as Northern European countries. Responsible executives or other persons rarely present strategy proposals.

Succession planning

Another factor is the potential loss of knowledge when changes in board membership occur. When members change there is a potential for the loss of valuable knowledge. However, change is good since it brings 'fresh blood' to the table. Boards in our survey tackled this problem in various ways. Most companies (78%) had a fixed term of tenure for their board members. For 46% of companies, the tenure was three years in length, for 18% it was five years, and for 16% it was four years. Shorter periods of one or two years, or periods of between six and 12 years were infrequent. Half of the boards allowed an unlimited number of re-elections for their members. In one-quarter of companies the board members can be re-elected up to six times (average 2.56 times). Other companies set other rules such as an age limit (10.6%), put into place a rotation plan according to certain specifications (for example, one-third of the board per annum), or they set a rule for re-elections dependent on the role of the member (inside director, independent director, etc.). In one board we observed, there was a limit of 12 years as the maximum time of duty. The election period was four years, so that the individual board member could be re-elected twice after serving his first term (which is what normally happened). Thus, on average, one-third of the board would be 'freshmen' (rarely women).

As illustrated by Figure 3.4, across all regions, formal procedures for nominating supervisory board members (73%) were more frequent than a set of written criteria for candidates (42%). In Anglo-Saxon countries, both were more frequent than in Northern Europe. Formal succession plans for CEO/chairmen were less common overall (globally 22%), but again were found significantly more often in Anglo-Saxon countries (35% versus 10% in Northern Europe).

Regular evaluations

Evaluations are another way to show commitment, since they demonstrate the willingness and courage to reflect on past work and to continuously improve the working style. However, a regular evaluation is still mostly

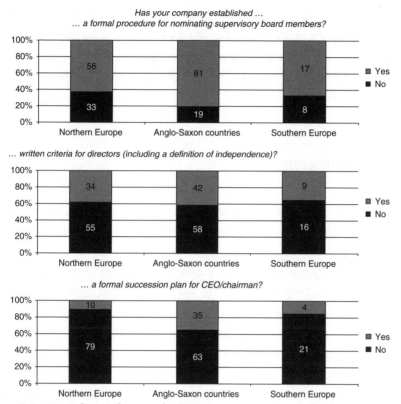

Figure 3.4   Formal procedures and criteria

practised for CEOs. One hundred and sixteen out of 232 companies reported a CEO evaluation process, as opposed to 69 companies that evaluated their chairman, 60 that evaluated the board as an entity and 52 that evaluated individual board members.

Board evaluations remain a sensitive issue, since many board members feel that their track record speaks for itself, illustrating the quality of their work. However, if the evaluations are carried out systematically and the process is designed and implemented in a way that all board members support, with confidentiality guaranteed, then individual board member evaluation is far less threatening and can bring big gains for the board as a group (see Chapter 7 by Fred Neubauer and Helga Krapf for more details).

External contacts

In our survey of investor relations representatives, we also enquired about external contacts of executive management and board of directors.

With regard to contacts with the financial community, respondents estimated the time (as a percentage of their total time) that CEOs, CFOs, non-executive chairmen or other board members spent with members of the financial community. Overall, CFOs spent an average of 13.5% of their time with members of the financial community, CEOs 9.2%, members of the board 4.4% and non-executive chairmen 3.4%. However, the range of answers was substantial. The CFOs spent up to 60% of their time, CEOs 45%, non-executive chairmen 30% and other members of the board 25% of their time with members of the financial community. Figure 3.5 shows the breakdown of average results per region.

In another question we asked whether members of the supervisory board spent time with other opinion leaders such as politicians, regulators, media, environmentalists or trade union leaders. We also asked how much time they spent with these other opinion leaders compared to the time spent with the financial community.

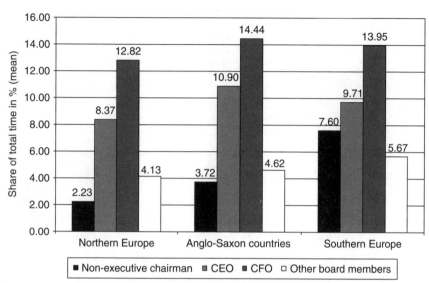

Figure 3.5 Time spent with members of the financial community, breakdown per region

The majority of companies (83.2%) reported contacts with opinion leaders. Figure 3.6 shows a breakdown of the comparison by regions. It seems that in Anglo-Saxon countries the willingness to spend time with other opinion leaders is less than in the other two regions. Altogether 60% of companies reported that 'less' than the financial community or even 'much less' time is spent with such persons. In Northern Europe 'less' was also the most frequently chosen option, more companies estimated at least 'equal' or even 'more'. In Southern Europe 'equal' was most frequently reported, but there was not such a clear difference to other alternatives as was the case in the other two regions.

This result has to be considered with some caution, especially since respondents were asked to estimate the time spent, perhaps a difficult task. And

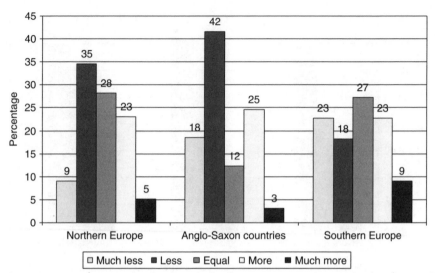

Figure 3.6 Time spent with opinion leaders in comparison with the financial community, by region

one must also not forget that board members have a wide range of representation duties and financial markets or other opinion leaders are just two of them. However, it shows that such contacts exist and again emphasizes the importance of the right information quality and quantity since such contacts contribute to a company's external image.

Who influences the board?

Finally, we tried to detect which stakeholder most influenced the board. The results can be found in Figure 3.7 and are not surprising: institutional investors lead by far. Based also on our interviews, we can assume that the exceptions are those companies where large individual shareholders account for 25–49% of the shares (in many countries, important corporate

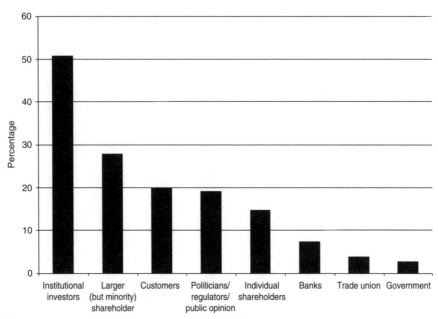

Figure 3.7   External influences on board decisions

decisions require a three-quarters majority and any holding of about 40%
ensures a majority at the annual general meeting). In any case, the board is
predominantly concerned with what shareholders want, if they know what
that is (see Chapter 5).

After looking at the broader picture and some statistics on how corporate
governance might work we analyse now what the specifics of a global
corporate governance system look like.

4
Managing Complexity in Global Corporate Governance

Global corporate governance dynamics: the case of DaimlerChrysler (DC)[1]

The development of the corporate governance of DaimlerChrysler is of special interest, since few companies make such an organizational leap to globalization in such a short time. At the time of the merger in 1998, Daimler-Benz was an export-oriented, predominantly German company, whereas Chrysler was focused almost exclusively on the US market. The merger of DaimlerChrysler brought new challenges, not common in acquisitions, and was soon followed by extension into Asia.

The main rationale of bringing together a company aimed at the US mass market and a German premium car company was consolidation in the global automotive industry. Today six groups account for approximately 85% of all sales. Both Daimler and Chrysler were seen as too small on their own, but they ranked number five merged together. Mercedes in particular had problems keeping its innovation proprietary, because suppliers only granted six months of exclusivity.

In terms of corporate governance criteria, it is interesting to look at the difference in involvement by the two boards in the pre-merger process. The CEO of Chrysler Bob Eaton informed his board as soon as he gave Jürgen Schrempp (CEO of Daimler-Benz) a positive response to merger talks. Schrempp, however, informed his management and supervisory board much later, when most decisions had already been made (see Figure 4.1 for details). This pattern reflects not only different leadership styles, but also different ways that boards can function (and how each system works). Whereas Eaton was consistently more cautious and sought consensus, Schrempp had a much tougher image due to his bold moves, contrary to stereotypes about dominant management styles in each culture. But beyond personalities, which are one of the four shaping factors of corporate governance (see Chapter 3), there are different ways that boards function. US boards tend to be smaller and more freewheeling: any issue can be brought up and discussed. The results of the discussion, however, are not always implemented. In contrast, boards of large German companies, be they management or supervisory boards, leave nothing to chance. Each agenda item is well prepared and documented with voluminous reports, with many people involved in the preparation and the results widely distributed to other organizational levels. In the case of DaimlerChrysler, as secrecy and speed were thought to be the key success factors of the merger's preparation, Schrempp was extremely concerned about any information leaks. In addition, legal provisions to protect corporate confidentiality in Germany are less deterring than in the US. It is therefore not a matter of employee representation on the supervisory board that can explain the different patterns.

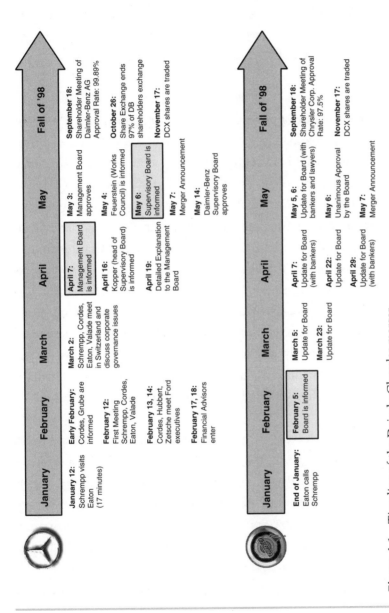

Figure 4.1 Timeline of the DaimlerChrysler merger

Source: Neubauer, Steger and Rädler (1999). Copyright © 1999 by IMD – International Institute for Management Development, Lausanne, Switzerland. All rights reserved. Not to be used or reproduced without written permission directly from IMD, Lausanne, Switzerland.

In contrast, the Post-Merger Integration (PMI) was shaped by the systematic thinking of German engineers (see Figure 4.2). Rüdiger Grube, the strategy mastermind of DaimlerChrysler, has a Ph.D. in aeronautic physics.

Each area was defined, an Issue Resolution Team (IRT) allocated and a hierarchical tree structure of projects set up, and supported by a PMI team. Each one of the approximately 1500 projects was tracked on a database, with a system to signal their status. However, as can be seen from the chart, a management board of 17 members is far too large to serve as a decision-making body. The small Chairman's Integration Council (six members plus the two chairmen of the management board) sorted out the numerous problems that surfaced along the way. The two board members, who served as sponsors for the IRTs, felt a need to delegate upwards, since they felt it was beyond their mandate. It should be further noted that the management board was really in the driver's seat. The supervisory board (including the shareholder committee) was less involved than independent board members presumably would have been at Chrysler. But as we will discuss later, would the different legal framework have made a difference if Chrysler had had the sheer size and complexity of DaimlerChrysler?

The 'Merger Made in Heaven', as it was frequently referred to, encountered serious problems. In any event, the car industry is one of the least favourite industries of financial analysts, characterized by capital intensity, highly specific assets, profit poisoning, persistent overcapacity, unionization and serious threat of commoditization. A narrow oligopoly is the most competitive market structure, where everybody watches everybody, and every competitive move triggers a countermove. All six big players followed a similar strategy. As a 'pure' car and commercial vehicle company (including

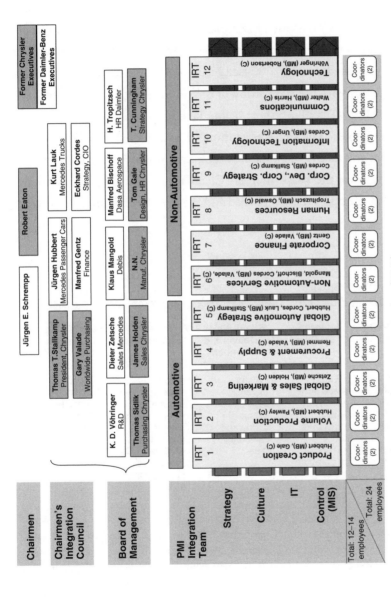

Figure 4.2 DaimlerChrysler's Post-Merger Integration (PMI)

the financial services arm) after the divestments of the rail, aerospace and other manufacturing divisions of Daimler-Benz, Chrysler and the commercial vehicle division did not turn out to be as strong as expected when the US market stagnated in mid-2000 (see Figure 4.3). The expansion into Asia was in full swing, with the acquisition of 37% of Mitsubishi Motors and 10% of Hyundai Motors, stopping short before having to consolidate the heavily indebted companies. The share price dropped from its (admittedly unrealistic) high level and followed companies such as GM and Ford, who were also not the darlings of the stock market. Calculations by investment bankers abounded that Chrysler was overpriced and the risks in Asia underestimated.

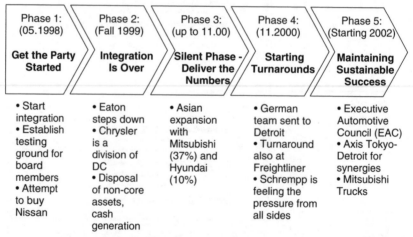

Figure 4.3 The five phases of DaimlerChrysler's turnaround
Source: Steger and Rädler (2003). Copyright © 2003 by IMD – International Institute for Management Development, Lausanne, Switzerland. All rights reserved. Not to be used or reproduced without written permission directly from IMD, Lausanne, Switzerland.

Surprisingly it was not the risk-averse Germans who sold the stock, but rather the American investors who dominantly profited from the merger as Chrysler's stockholders. From an equal shareholding between Europe and the US at the time of the merger, DaimlerChrysler is now a majority-owned German company (57%, the US 14%, Europe 21%). However, the majority of shareholders are institutional investors (54%), whereas retail investors account for 27%, plus the larger shareholders Emirate of Kuwait and Deutsche Bank with approximately 7% and 12% respectively.

But the way corporate governance developed was, in our analysis, more influenced by the business development than by the shift in investors. The Chairman's Integration Council ceased to exist in September 1999 when Eaton wanted to step down (maybe knowing where Chrysler was heading). The Automotive Council, set up to coordinate between divisions as a successor to the Integration Council, in addition to the management board, was not regarded as very successful. This was due not solely to the organizational set-up, but also to the limited synergy potential between Mercedes and Chrysler. The Commercial Vehicles Division did not cooperate with Mercedes either. Due to the different car designs and to protect the price premium of the Mercedes brand, no shared platforms, motors, etc. were advisable (with some minor exceptions and some economies of scale in commodity parts needed for cars). This changed when Mitsubishi Motors and Hyundai came to the DaimlerChrysler Group. Now a clearly positioned premium brand could deliver new technology in a controlled, time-staggered manner, while volume brands reaped the economies of scale of standardized components, common sourcing, shared platforms and a world engine (with 1.5 million units planned for 2005).

This required real decision-making power by the new Executive Automotive Committee (EAC) and continuity of work (organized by the Strategy Department). The EAC was alternately chaired by the CEO Schrempp and Jürgen Hubbert, CEO of Mercedes-Benz. For legal and cultural reasons, the coordination between Mitsubishi and Hyundai happened in the Alliance Committee, which worked in a similar pattern and with preparation by the same Corporate Strategy Department. Additionally, the Commercial Vehicle Division set up the same mechanisms for the integration of the Mercedes, Freightliner and Fuso brands and better integration between the different segments.

Another committee that was dissolved was the shareholder committee. It had originally been modelled on the US-style board of directors, with the two chairmen of the management board, all ten shareholder representatives and four outsiders (former Chrysler directors, who were not on the Daimler-Chrysler supervisory board). This committee had no formal decision-making power, since this rested with the supervisory board. Its mission was rather to 'restrict itself to debate and counselling and provide fact-based recommendations to support opinion forming among the shareholder representatives', according to CFO Gentz. It is not uncommon in the German system of codetermination that the two benches (shareholder and labour) meet separately before the session and then together conduct it 'like an opera' (as one US observer put it). However, a special committee at the supervisory level for this purpose was seen as unnecessary, once the DaimlerChrysler integration process was routine and US citizens continued to serve on the supervisory board (most of them former Chrysler directors). The labour committee continued for another reason: by the codetermination law only German employees can elect their representatives for the supervisory board (clearly an anachronism in a global company). This meant that the US workforce is underrepresented, with only one US labour representative serving on the union contingent to the DaimlerChrysler board. The labour committee allows foreign employees at least to make their voices heard.

The shareholder committee was replaced by the Chairman's Council. The council is chaired by the CEO Jürgen Schrempp and consists of six shareholder representatives of the supervisory board (including its chairman, Hilmar Kopper) and five external members who are all either CEOs or chairmen of global companies (including the chairman of Mitsubishi Corporation, still an important shareholder in Mitsubishi Motors). In an official statement, the complementary task of the chairman's council was described as to:

> provide advice to management on global business strategy issues. Elements of American and European corporate governance structures are combined to meet the specific requirements of a truly global company and the interests of the different stakeholders. . . The legal rights and responsibilities of the Supervisory Board will remain untouched.

The now 11 members of the management board are invited to the Chairman's Council when issues within their scope of responsibility are discussed. The corporate strategy department also does most of the preparation.

Together with the International Advisory Board, which already existed in Daimler-Benz as a sounding board for global developments, the current corporate governance structure is illustrated in Figure 4.4.

Figure 4.5 summarizes the briefly described parallelism of business development in the process of becoming a global company on the one side, and the evolution of the corporate governance structure on the other, which is further discussed in the next chapter.

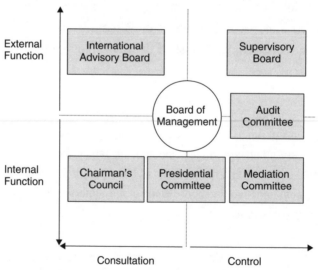

Figure 4.4 DaimlerChrysler's corporate governance structure
Source: Steger and Rädler (2003). Copyright © 2003 by IMD – International Institute for Management Development, Lausanne, Switzerland. All rights reserved. Not to be used or reproduced without written permission directly from IMD, Lausanne, Switzerland.

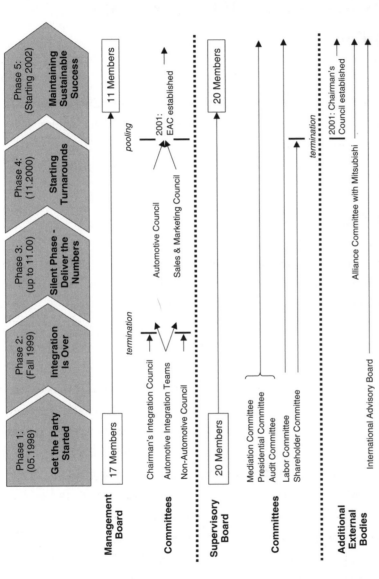

Figure 4.5 The development of business and corporate governance structure at DaimlerChrysler, 1998–2002

Lessons learned for global corporate governance

There are general lessons that can be learned from DaimlerChrysler. Similar issues and features can be found in many other companies, which have deployed their assets around the globe, especially if they want to escape the narrow dominance of their national corporate governance paradigm.

Lesson 1: 'Learn as you go'

There is no fixed template for global corporate governance, especially if one focuses on more than just legal compliance. Of course, this is in itself a tricky issue and covers some of the following areas:

- The different legal configuration of the board: individual responsibility in the US (which is why, for example, CEOs and CFOs have to certify the released numbers) versus the collective responsibility of boards as organs of a company, which is a legal person in its own right (and therefore all members have to sign off the books). This leads to very different (personal) liability risk, and as a result, insurance premiums.
- Disclosure requirements differ widely as do accounting rules. As the management saying goes: 'profit is an opinion, only cash is a fact'.
- The appointment of auditors is under German law the right of the Annual General Assembly. In the US, it is the obligation of the Audit Committee, not least because generally in the US the legal rights of the Annual General Meeting are less than those in Europe.

- As employees do not count as independent, a codetermined German supervisory board can never have a majority of independent directors, which runs counter to the whole idea of a supervisory board that is separated from (top) management.

The list could continue, but as we have argued above extensively, corporate governance is more than compliance with the law. It needs to provide value added in strategy formulation, as well as in monitoring and controlling the strategy implementation, and in evaluating and selecting the leadership of a company. But here corporate governance on a global scale faces the third dilemma, which we have already discussed in Chapter 2: the complexity of a global company with different axes of management (for example: global product lines, regions, key accounts, functions, projects). DaimlerChrysler as a car company is relatively simple compared to more diversified giants such as Nestlé, Unilever, P&G, Bayer, DuPont, Shell, BP, HP, etc. On the one hand, corporate governance has to match the complexity such that there is no structural and organizational rupture between the corporation and its governance structure. On the other hand, there is a risk that the work within the governance institutions will be overwhelmed by the complexity.

DaimlerChrysler, like many others, tried to find a way of avoiding this through a design, which in our analysis is based on specialization and delegation. The specialization could be seen in the committees or councils, which evolved during the process of globalization. For example, in the division of labour between the Chairman's Council and the supervisory board, it is plausible to assume that the first focuses on the strategy contribution, whereas the latter looks more at the compliance side and has the final say in electing the members of the management board. Similarly, it can be assumed that the Executive Automotive Council details the product strategy, which is the dominant strategy component in an automobile company, whereas the full management board is more concerned with functional aspects relevant to the whole company (e.g. finance, HR). But as much as decentralization is one of the few levers to effectively manage complexity, it also has its drawbacks. Without a strong leader, it can release too many centrifugal forces, leading to internal politics, inconsistency, duplication of efforts, etc. This is probably the reason why in Northern Europe *de facto* CEOs emerged, although by law the board of management is in its totality responsible and all members are formally equal. But as everybody knew: some are more equal than others.

Given the complexity, one size cannot fit all. A corporate governance system that serves all three purposes under the conditions of a global company has to be designed. These three purposes are (1) measuring compliance of corporate governance, (2) selecting and monitoring a top team, and (3) value-added input to corporate evolutions, especially in terms of strategy design and implementation.

Lesson 2: Becoming global – the hour of the executives

Despite the public's high hopes of the miracles that independent directors on any board can achieve, it is evident that power (and with that the responsibility) shifts to the full-time executives. Just look at the range of risks any board has to deal with in a company similar to DaimlerChrysler:

- Currency risk: if you sell in several dozen markets of differing importance, contagious financial crisis can easily multiply country risks. Currently Latin America is the hotspot – but for how long?

- Financial services risks: as DaimlerChrysler (among others) learned, the financial services division is a source of profit, but also of massive risk, since it allows operational management to buy market share today at the cost of future earnings when the risk materializes. For example, residual values of leasing contracts were estimated too high relative to the market price for a used car when the contract expired, incurring a loss.

- Technology risk: should DaimlerChrysler accelerate the fuel-cell technology to substitute the combustion engine or not? With which fuel (for example, natural gas or hydrogen)? What about diesel particle filters, fuel efficiency, 'drive by wire', lightweight materials, already relevant for tomorrow's cars? Missing one means suffering for half a decade.

- Risk of product liability and warranty: the former, a nightmare in the US, the latter a trade-off between accelerated market introduction and maturity of new technology or designs, currently especially in electronics.

- Risks to the multiple brands, either due to incorrect product positioning or contagion of mishaps from one brand to another.

- Exit risks due to asset specificity (e.g. high cost of factory closures).

- Legal risks due to contradicting legal requirements (e.g. some of the affirmative action programmes in the US could be seen as discrimination in other legal contexts).

- Residual risks that nobody had even dreamt about before they happened (e.g. the $8 billion Kekorian lawsuit over the merger of equals).

Consider the range of risk management issues as just one set of issues to be dealt with, with the specific knowledge, limited resources and time, as well as other constraints, such as the pressure of a consensus, of any independent board member. Whether it is a one-tier or a two-tier board is of little importance. This dynamic is not unique to companies: in politics the shift of power from parliament to the executive has long been debated. This makes it even more important for boards to focus (as discussed in Chapter 2) on the process and system design, the internal checks and balances (e.g. bold CEO balanced by a strong CFO) and to raise more pertinent questions than to try to provide answers. But in any case, we have to be realistic about our expectations of boards.

Lesson 3: You cannot be everybody's darling

Expectations of corporate governance, as discussed in Chapter 1, are currently running high, probably too high, and they have become volatile. 'Focus only on your core business' was the battle cry not too long ago. Today greater risk diversification is appreciated. The role of the chairman and CEO should be separated. Novartis, which is generally regarded as an example of best practice in corporate governance, got bad press when it combined the two roles (but appointed a lead director). Not too long ago, however, the common US practice of job integration was praised as good for bold decisions (in contrast to the European consensus wimps). Currently DaimlerChrysler is criticized for not publishing the individual salaries and benefits of its board members. The list can go on indefinitely. Given the many stakeholders (or sometimes only commentators), their widely differing interests and perspectives (and sometimes also their short memories), it is impossible for any global company to be everybody's darling in their corporate governance practice or in any other area. What is needed more than before is an explanation of why the company's board has decided on certain issues the way they did. To create transparency and deliver reasoning is the only way to limit the degree of criticism (and its potential impact) that is currently pouring over companies.

But there are some nagging questions in the corporate world, which go far beyond the fashion-driven public outcry.

5
Some Nagging Questions

The first question is about the missing shareholder. It is sometimes noted that shareholders are the 'missing link' in corporate
governance. After all, the board is the representative of the shareholders, regardless of whether or not it considers other stakeholders (whereas
in practice the difference is probably not as great as it appears to be in the
academic and political debate). What do shareholders want? And who is the
shareholder?

In today's world, more often than not, institutional investors buy the
shares and allocate them to funds, which are owned by individuals or other
institutions. But here again we run into what is at the heart of the corporate
governance paradigm: the principal–agent problem. Fund managers invest,
for example in the case of a mutual fund, with the money of Joe Miller in
Kentucky or Hans Müller in Bavaria. Are their interests aligned with those of
their clients? Funds are measured by their performance relative to other funds
or benchmarks (although the asset management industry is trying to reduce
the transparency of such comparisons), which requires unrestricted trading.
Any longer-term involvement – especially a seat on the board – would trigger
a great deal of insider-trading rules and restrictions. Especially when funds

are indexing (in other words, buying all securities in an index proportionally, for example blue chips as DAX 50, DOW 30, or sector specifics such as the European Chemical Industry), they need not be concerned with the corporate governance structure, because the potential economic impact of corporate governance balances out in the selected portfolio.

It should be noted here that the empirical evidence that investors pay a premium for good corporate governance refers to the differences between developing countries and OECD countries, not nuances between corporate governance systems in companies in one developed country, all complying with the same laws and regulations. So the Russian oil company Yukos can generate a share premium for its significantly greater transparency and better governance than 'normal' Russian companies, but DuPont cannot similarly generate a share premium over, for example, GM.

Furthermore, asset managers rarely challenge companies when there is cross-dependence. Cross-dependence occurs when a fund or an affiliate also manages the pension fund of the company. For example, in Germany, frequently when bankers were on the supervisory board of a company, that company was a good credit client. Until recently the funds run by banks were definitely hampered in any watchdog activity. When the share position is difficult to exit (e.g. due to general market conditions or the narrow market) fund managers are concerned that their efforts to improve the corporate governance system will first drive the share price down. In small countries with a closed, homogeneous elite any public criticism could be easily regarded as 'politically incorrect'. No small wonder that corporate governance activities by funds were selective at best and often related to phases of market decline (with the additional US speciality that the public employee funds – CalPERs, TIAA-CREF – were relatively more proactive).

Another set of proxies eager to position themselves as representatives of the shareholders are investment bankers. Although its credibility has recently suffered, the very business model of investment banking allows it to represent at best a fraction of shareholders. Investment bankers' lifeblood is dealing, which requires volatility: the more volatility, the more buying and selling. 'Widows and orphans' investments were therefore pushed aside with contempt, although they serve the need of an important segment of stockholders. Furthermore, due to the drive for share buyback, investment banks often increased the risk for bondholders, since companies became more leveraged (and the risk of default increased).

For the retail investor at the individual level, his or her opportunity cost points to the 'exit' direction, rather than the 'voice' direction: i.e. if he or she gets involved ('voices' his or her concern), his or her influence is marginal. The effort required to inform him or herself of complicated issues and to act is relatively high compared to the gain he or she might achieve. For the same reason, web-based voting does not solve the problem of low shareholder representation. The difficulties of organizing small shareholders into associations, who collectively represent the small fry at the general meeting, carry their own principal–agent problems and few are interested. Currently, small shareholders tend to move more to other forms of investment and avoid equity before trying to exercise their property rights.

So, where does that leave us? The irony is that the more widely dispersed equity is in a population (e.g. in the Anglo-Saxon countries relative to continental Europe, where stockholding remains more concentrated), the more difficult it is for shareholders to express the preferences, both in terms of corporate governance practice and the direction of the company, leaving the boards guessing and without any effective control. The famous question 'Who guards the guardian?' cannot be answered under the current circumstances for widely held public companies.

The other nagging question relates to the conditions under which management cuts corners. Economists believe for better or worse that (most) people behave according to the incentives set (as the manager joke goes: 'the bad news is, you get what you reward'). One big, perhaps the biggest, incentive to massage the numbers was that stock markets were driven not by facts, but rather by deviation from expectations (reflected in the so-called analyst consensus on quarterly earnings). To deviate from these expectations was for the most part bad for the share price, even when it was good news. Investment bankers don't like surprises that make them look bad and ignorant. So the game was to meet expectations. And US companies succeeded: defying all statistical probability of deviation that can be expected in a sample such as the share indexes, the vast majority made the numbers.

The bad news is that the expectations of the analysts were greater than what the real economy could deliver. Especially towards the end of the bubble, there were growing statistical differences between the profit that companies reported and the profit numbers in the national accounts. Companies delayed booking expenses and brought forward booking revenues. On a suitable occasion, a big, extraordinary, one-time item generated a huge loss in one quarter and the game could start anew, this time on a lower level upon which the consensus growth rates were calculated. And all this despite (or because of?) the multitude of GAAP rules, but relatively risk-free if the consensus is managed over time, since investment bankers already look forward, never back.

Has this changed? Despite some regulatory corrections, which eliminated the most egregious rip-off of customers that occurred during the bubble, we remain unsure as to whether the basic pattern prevails. We have seen too many attempts to drive up the stock prices again just by spreading good news. If our pessimistic assumption holds true, then the next accounting scandal is merely a question of time. (While the case of Health South may still be the legacy of the old system, the next situation where earnings are overstated cannot be blamed on the past.)

But maybe all players have learned from the past and are behaving more responsibly and intelligently than in the past. The first step would be for short-term stock price fluctuations to no longer make boards nervous or penalize managers via incentive structures that gamble on volatility. The second would be to put the structures of corporate governance into the context of the more important questions that need to be addressed.

Part II

Three Burning Questions for Boards

6
The Role and Responsibilities of the CEO[1]

Peter Lorange

Introduction

Consider the following: 'The current board reforms to strengthen and "empower" boards at the expense of the CEO will make boards more rather than less significant agents' (Tainio, Lilja and Santalainen, 2001, p. 443). The question, however, is what *is* the role of the CEO relative to the board? And what are his/her responsibilities relative to the board? Should we see this as a win–lose relationship? Or, would it be more meaningful to consider the board and the CEO as being on the same team, and to look for win–win relationships? These are the issues we shall try to shed light on in this chapter (Carter and Lorsch, 2003, pp. 59–84).

As a starting observation we can safely say that clearly the CEO now needs to understand better than ever *who* the owners of the company are. This would include key institutional owners as well. In general, we see more ownership-based influence, and more active boards today, with more power relative to the CEO. Boards have become more energetic! The institutional investor movement has certainly played a role here. And special interest groups such as those pushing for, say, ecological considerations are also increasingly being heard. Another reason we have seen a swing toward increased power of the board has to do with the dysfunctional behaviour of the CEOs in several prominent corporations (*Wall Street Journal*, 2003). We have witnessed the demise of once great companies such as Enron, under Derek Lay; WorldCom, under Bernie Ebbers; Tyco, under Dennis Kozlowski; Conseco, under Stephen Hilbert; and Adelphia, under John Ragas – to mention just a few. While all of these are US based, prominent non-US corporations in the same situation include Skandia, under Lars-Erik Petterson, Crédit Suisse under Lukas Mühlemann and Swissair under Philippe Bruggisser. For an in-depth discussion of the Swissair case, see Chapter 2.

We do not, however, find it useful simply to accept this shift of the balance of power toward the board and away from the CEO. The more relevant question is: 'What is a pragmatically workable balance?' (Strebel, 2003, p. 27; George, 2003, p. 173). To better understand the role and responsibilities of the CEO, we shall claim that it is key *first* to appreciate several underlying essential elements in corporate governance which might in turn help us to determine a meaningful mandate for the CEO in various circumstances. Particularly vital are the following questions: 'How can the truly important decisions for the company be made as correctly as possible?' and 'What *are* the truly critical decisions?' They typically have to do with each particular company vis-à-vis its specific business environment – its competitive context. Again, I would refer to Chapter 2 where a set of company-specific influencing factors is delineated. It is thus key to understand in what particular type of company the CEO operates. The CEO's role relative to the board is different in a bank than in a typical industrial conglomerate or in a major shipping company.

It is thus *not* a matter of delineating the board's responsibilities and roles by following a standard set of prescriptions, such as for instance those contained in reports, such as the Cadbury Report (UK), the Smith Report (UK) or the Noerby Report (Denmark), or prescribed in legislation, such as Sarbanes-Oxley (US). Nor is it a matter of accepting the often poor behaviour of many CEOs (see the examples above) as a reason to scale down the CEO's power relative to the board. Clearly the law must be followed when it comes to practising responsibility for control, primarily in order to safeguard the firm. Beyond this, however, the key question should be *how* fundamental proactive decision making can be practised in order to guide what is best for the firm. And the relative responsibilities of the board and the CEO must be outlined in light of this key question – and with the realization that they are essentially on the *same* team!

This means that the CEO and the board must be able to identify the types of key decisions that are a true *must* for *this* company, and then above all follow up on these. To zoom in on these key questions, the CEO should perhaps attempt to structure his/her decision making relative to the board by focusing above all on these three general areas:

- Setting goals, objectives and strategic plans,
- Setting budgets, and
- Post-facto approving the key actions and the accounts.

The CEO should initiate these, but the board must be involved in shaping the key decisions here. It should be an iterative process.

In the first two cases, key decisions should be built into plans and budgets, and systematically discussed by the board, as far as possible, again by focusing on what is critical for the company. Also for key post-facto approvals should the board *and* the CEO be involved? We shall discuss examples of how the CEO takes the lead vis-à-vis the board – as a proactive catalyst – regarding these issues later in the chapter.

The board, in contrast, must also take a proactive stance, a lead in delineating what *it* sees as key decisions where the board needs to be involved, versus daily operating decisions for which the CEO should be responsible on his/her own. It must also identify the types of decisions and issues it expects to be kept informed about, so that board members are always likely to have up-to-date and relevant background to deal with a given issue when it arises.

As the opening paragraph of this chapter suggests, some have portrayed the issue as a trade-off between the CEO's power and the board's power. In this regard, Pearce and Zahra (1991), for instance, have proposed the conceptual scheme shown in Figure 6.1.

Reviewing Pearce and Zahra's framework, one might gain the impression that there is a conflict between the board and the CEO. We shall claim the contrary. The board *and* the CEO need to implement the key success factors for the firm *together*. There should be no conflict between the board and the CEO. The key is what the CEO and the board as one team can do for the company!

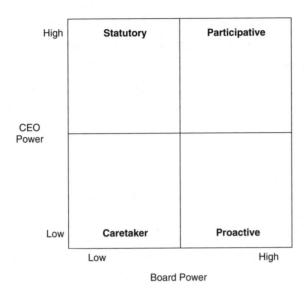

Figure 6.1 CEO's power versus the board's power
Source: Pearce and Zahra, 1991. © John Wiley & Sons Limited. Reproduced with permission

The way in which this *balance* of interaction between the board and CEO takes place may, however, differ from firm to firm. Let us consider this balance between the board and the CEO in two extreme settings: a major shipping company on the one hand and a major bank on the other. In a major shipping company, the board can only lay out the general premises behind its strategy, such as general attitude toward risk-taking, overall diversity of the firm, etc., and must to a large extent delegate the actual decision making to the CEO. The reason for this is the need for rapid, opportunistic decision making to take advantage of the global shipping markets and rapid execution thereafter. The board can outline the overall context in which this must take place, but it is the CEO and his/her associates who will have to ask the questions, 'What is this market-based deal all about?' and 'What shall we decide on relative to the market here?' and then draw on the relevant expertise to support this. It is typically vital to have no delays, which can often be expensive, or the deal may have gone all together. Since tempo and speed are so critical, relevant initiatives regarding key decisions must largely come from the CEO. The board can only ask to be kept informed within the overall general parameters and limitations that have been set for the CEO.

At the other extreme, consider the case of a major bank. Here the board will typically play a rather active role in each major credit commitment decision, indeed on a project-by-project basis. This is set out by law, and it is thus mandatory for the board to be centrally involved in this credit allocation. With the implementation of the so-called Basle II Convention as of 2005 the board may, in all likelihood, become even more heavily involved! It should, however, be pointed out here that it is critical *not* to let these legal requirement issues kill the successful functioning of a relationship between a board and a CEO. Thus, compliance with the law is one thing, and must of course be respected. At the same time, however, it might be possible for the board and the CEO to have a different type of balance between themselves on other key issues. One might have a strong board and a strong CEO, but with shifting the board/CEO balance, with strong board power relative to the CEO when it comes to credit approval issues, as well as a more balanced board/CEO equilibrium with both a strong board and a strong CEO when it comes to other issues. Pearce and Zahra might describe this as partly proactive, partly participative. In contrast, one would say that the board of the shipping company would be of a more statutory variety. None of these archetypes of balance between the CEO and the board are better than the others *per se*. What is important is that the balance between the two entities is reached based on what is best for the company, in terms of dealing with the company's key issues.

It is also essential for the board to act as a *team* and for the CEO to interact with the board as a single entity, not on a one-to-one basis. The CEO should try to treat the board in a non-political way, as opposed to attempting to create one-to-one side deals. The board should be a *resource* for the CEO, again helping him/her to focus on what is best for the company. Occasionally the board might of course overrule the CEO, but hopefully the CEO can accept this in the spirit of 'good must always be done even better'. The CEO might indeed see him or herself as being before the board for an exam at each meeting. And this might lead to even better decisions. The CEO will not be hampered by unfounded prestige considerations: no egg-on-the-face, no hurt feelings! As an illustration of how this can go wrong, see the discussion of the 'War at the Helm of Elicore' case in Chapter 9. It also follows that once decisions have been made, they must be loyally acted upon by all board members and the CEO, despite any difference of opinion that might have existed, again without any politics.

Even though we must consider the board and the CEO as one team, we can still argue that in some cases the CEO is perhaps the most critical person after all, the *primus inter pares*. One can perhaps further argue that the chairman of the board is the next most important person. If these two can work well together, then much contribution towards good value creation can be resolved.

A key role for board members is to constantly ask themselves whether the company has the right CEO. Again this is one agenda item where the board members and CEO will not have the same roles on the team. Is the CEO focusing on the right issues? Is he/she tackling the right challenges and problems? As Dotlich and Cairo (2003, p. 149) state, 'Companies frequently experience serious setbacks when entire groups of people (i.e. the board) collude to overlook, deny or manage around a CEO's negative personality characteristics.' Thus, the board must play a proactive role in spotting the CEO's potential lack of performance. One must further expect that the CEO will not mask his/her performance relative to the board. The board must critically look into a CEO's potential failure to execute a turnaround (Stopford and Baden-Fuller, 1990); establish a success track (Tainio and Valpola, 1996); bounce ideas off the board (Lorsch and MacIver, 1989); allow the board to evaluate strategic proposals (Lorsch, 1995); and allow the board to be part of shaping critical actions (McNulty and Pettigrew, 1999). The board should definitely look at the CEO's performance when it comes to all of these issues.

It goes without saying that this is not only a matter of the CEO's performance – but it also requires an active, open-minded attitude from the board members. Consider the statement of Saatchi & Saatchi CEO Kevin Roberts regarding the board: 'The average age is 10 years on the path and experience is pretty similar. Generally speaking, they are don't-rock-the-boat guys at the end of their careers, who have been there, done that ... aren't driven or hungry anymore and ... haven't seen a customer for so long, they are totally out of touch with what the company is trying to sell' (quoted in Finkelstein, 2003, p. 203). Clearly it will be hard for boards with this type of membership to be effective sparring partners for the CEO, or for it to provide an appropriate and effective assessment of the CEO.

Let us now review four types of issue that the CEO must deal with relative to the board: substantive strategic leadership issues, issues dictated by the law, issues dealing with professional organizational development, as well as the issue of economic independence of the board members relative to the company they serve. It should again be pointed out that in each case the actual interchange between the CEO and the board will be dictated by what is critical for *this* company, in *this* particular setting, referring also to the Pearce and Zahra (1991) framework (see Figure 6.1).

Substantive strategic leadership issues for the CEO

A first professional expectation for the board to have with regard to the CEO is for him/her to develop a strategic plan. He/she should here emphasize *both* long-term, 'top line' performance *and* the short-term, 'bottom line'. This is a balancing act – not a trade-off – and it must be carefully discussed with the board – and clearly understood by all. And, the strategy is to *be prepared*, so that one can act fast when the opportunity arises! A useful way to deal with this challenge is to consider a particular business area, and portray the various activities in this business area along the lines delineated in Figure 6.2 (Chakravarthy and Lorange, 2004).

Some of the activities in a particular business area will consist of focusing on the existing business, in terms of both established markets and proven competences, and this *protect and extend* strategic activity will typically lead

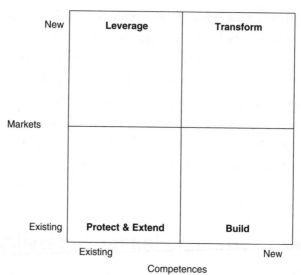

Figure 6.2   The CEO's strategic paradigm
Source: Chakravarthy and Lorange, 2004

to (hopefully) steady bottom-line results. If the company attempts to develop new markets through building on its strengths in this business area, it may then be able to *leverage* on these competences relatively easily. For instance, it can take its successes into new markets, say new countries, thereby creating longer-term growth, but without necessarily causing too much of a drain on the bottom line. Further, it can *build* new competences, adding them to the present strengths. This can also involve resources and require a longer-term focus, but the idea again would be to make sure that the *build* activities are realistic when it comes to adhering to the long-term/short-term balance for the firm. Finally, we have the *transform* activities, which are clearly long term. These must not be allowed to absorb resources to the extent that they become a threat to the short-term bottom-line results. The CEO might want to build his/her strategic plan around a framework such as this one, in order to secure *both* growth *and* profits – and the board must be fully with him/her on this.

Let us consider the CEO of ISS (Integrated Service Solutions – one of the world's largest cleaning services companies) and relate his situation to this strategic agenda. Traditionally ISS might have been seen largely as a multiple country-based company with activities in cleaning, a rather mature set of businesses, typically having a healthy short-term cash flow. But the growth side was missing! The CEO therefore spearheaded several initiatives to make ISS a more multi-service-oriented company, with higher value added and more long-term growth potential. Partly he did this through the so-called 'business build' initiatives, to accumulate new competences in three areas: pest control, clean rooms and damage control. These strategic initiatives were thus to *build* for growth! Partly he initiated several acquisitions, including that of Abilis, a large French company that was heavily involved in several complementary fields, including landscaping. This was a new business platform for ISS. The CEO was quickly able to leverage on Abilis's landscaping activities by introducing landscaping more broadly into the already existing multi-country organizations. This was an example of a leverage strategy, which also enhanced growth. The board advised and appraised the CEO regarding each of these strategic developments, but was not driving the strategy itself. The strategic initiatives came from the CEO and the organization. This is consistent with Lorsch and McIver's findings (Lorsch and McIver, 1989), as well as with those of Steger (see Chapter 3 regarding the roles of the board in strategy setting).

A second issue for the CEO to delineate, together with the board, is the *number* of *business platforms* that should be present in the firm's overall portfolio strategy. How widely should a firm be spreading itself, and what should the relationship between these business areas be? For instance, the board of Norsk Hydro, working with the CEO, agonized for a long time over whether it would be best from a shareholder value creation point of view to maintain Norsk Hydro's three unrelated business platforms: oil and gas, light metals and agricultural products. It was widely felt that the stock market was heavily discounting the Norsk Hydro stock, seeing it as relatively unattractive for stockholders to own shares in what the market saw as an unrelated conglomerate such as this. Finally, the CEO and the board decided to spin off the agricultural business as a separate entity, focusing the firm on two unrelated business platforms rather than three.

Another example can be found in the shipping company I. M. Skaugen. Traditionally this company had activities in classical bulk shipping, large crude oil tankers, ferries (Color Line) and gas carriers. All of these business platforms were generally positioned in rather mature business segments. I. M. Skaugen's CEO, with the support of his board, initiated a restructuring of the company, largely through divestitures and acquisitions, which resulted in three interrelated business platforms:

- The Aframax Crude Oil Tanker business, which included lighterage,[2] which carried crude oil up the large Mississippi River basin in the US. This required a strategy with heavy emphasis on *build*, in the sense that the necessary new competences would have to be put together to carry out the key activities within this broad logistics-based value chain.
- A gas ship pool, initially in global trade, but then with a specific focus on China's coastal waters, i.e. a *leverage* strategy, in which the general gas business transportation know-how was leveraged geographically.

- A gas transportation lighterage, on the Yangtze River in China, which built on I. M. Skaugen's combined capabilities from the US lighterage business and from the coastal Chinese gas transportation business. This was a *transform* strategy.

In this instance, we can see that although Skaugen's three business platforms are largely independent of one another from a cash flow point of view, and in terms of which macroeconomic conditions they rely on, they are still highly interrelated when it comes to the competences and processes that they draw on. These are the types of issues that the CEO must share with the board.

Third, the CEO must have a clear handle on the issue of understanding major risks as part of the firm's strategy, and this is an area where he/she and the board also need to work closely together. Let us give an example here, namely that of the industrial conglomerate Kvaerner A/S, when it was acquiring Trafalgar House in 1996 (Hamilton and Ohlsson, 2000). At the time, Kvaerner was in rather mature businesses, with perhaps too much emphasis on classical mechanical industries. Thus, it potentially stood to gain a lot from acquiring an asset with more growth-oriented businesses, such as those of Trafalgar House. The acquisition did, however, involve taking on a lot of debt – perhaps too much in retrospect and with too high a risk. The company became too vulnerable to downturns in revenues later on, with a much higher breakeven point, and this made the successful running of the company difficult. At the end, both the board and the CEO had to leave!

A fourth issue has to do with understanding the often diverse but hopefully honest sentiments of the stakeholders, particularly when it comes to mergers and acquisitions. The board must make sure that the CEO masters the overall chemistry issues here. Let us again give an example: in 1997, Royal Caribbean Cruise Lines acquired Celebrity Cruises. The stakeholder issues were well understood. The majority owner of Celebrity became a member of the Royal Caribbean board, and the two organizations were set up in such a way that they represented separate ongoing entities, separate growth platforms within the cruise industry, but with some selective consolidations in the operations area where particular synergies could be achieved. Subsequently, however, when Royal Caribbean attempted to acquire Princess Cruises from P&O it ran into problems, perhaps above all when it failed to fully understand the key stakeholders in their board and upper management. Also, Royal Caribbean's own board was perhaps not as eager as its own upper management to provide a 'sweet' deal. Eventually, Royal Caribbean's archcompetitor Carnival Cruises took over Princess – a major blow. The issue of how well top management was able to analyse, understand and manage key stakeholder issues – on both sides – could be questioned here. In general, achieving total clarity regarding stakeholders' positions should be an issue of concern for the board in cases of major acquisitions and/or divestitures.

Issues a CEO must deal with, as required by law

It is clear that the law in many countries is becoming increasingly specific about what constitutes critical governance issues, and is requiring that such issues be handled accordingly by *both* the board and the CEO. The CEO must of course fully support the board in this regard. This is an attempt to legislate safe governance, including protecting the interests of normal investors as well as society at large. It is clear that the CEO must proactively respect all of the relevant laws and give his/her full support to them. He/she must help the board to comply and also represent the corporation forcefully in all such compliance matters.

In many instances there is also a protocol for the board regarding the various compliance issues that affect the company, such as pollution control, safety, etc. It is useful for the CEO to initiate – vis-à-vis the board – a review of these issues at least once per year, again to look for ways to 'make good even better'.

Professional management issues

Today's professional CEO should also be expected to take a stance when it comes to various professional management issues. Here the board must expect the CEO to perform at least up to normal professional standards. A key issue would be organizational development, to build a better corporate performance. As part of this, the CEO must be expected to create a true organizational learning culture. Here again, the board may play an important role, in the sense that organizational learning should also be part of the board's agenda too, so that it can also constantly improve its understanding of the truly critical issues facing the firm. Zahra and Pearce (1989) have found that when there is such an active attitude toward organizational learning on the part of the board, these organizations tend to be more oriented toward high performance.

A second issue for the CEO would be to have some, at least rudimentary, succession plans in place. This is particularly true in case of 'working accidents', so that others can step in (perhaps only on an interim basis) to take over the CEO's own position as well as other senior management positions. Here it should be clear, however, that it is the board that appoints the new CEO, not the CEO who appoints a successor. Still, the board should expect that contingency-based succession planning be in place to safeguard the operations of a company in case of unforeseen events.

As part of this, the board must expect the CEO to carry out performance appraisals of his key people, and to reward them with incentives based on performance. It goes without saying that the CEO's own performance should be appraised by the board, again based as much as possible on actual results delivered. However, the professional CEO should show moderation when it comes to pushing for his/her own compensation. The relationship between the way the CEO is incentivized and the compensation and bonuses awarded to the rest of the top management in the company should be reasonable. Here again, it is vital that the excesses we have seen recently when it comes to CEO compensation are eliminated. The CEO should be expected to exercise professional judgement here. A pragmatic, realistic dialogue on this is needed between the board and the CEO.

Independence

We know that the board of directors must be independent. No special interest group should dominate the board. Cronyism should be avoided. We know that special committees should probably be avoided too, to prevent the formation of sub-units within the board, which could potentially create an environment in which politicking thrives. The board should be one team of all independent members, who should be compensated for their ability to contribute to the success of the firm in their own ways but, again, at a reasonable level. They must indeed be expected to speak up, and not be held hostage by the company itself due to economic and/or other dependencies on it.

The same is of course true for the CEO. Herein lies one of the political roots of the problem regarding CEO performance that is widely perceived today, as Finkelstein (2003, pp. 41–43) states:

> Hired hands – let's call them CEOs – have incentives that are different from stockholders, whose interests run more into return on investment and shareholder value than individual pay and prestige. This so-called principal/agent problem can occur when managers (the agents) act more in their own self-interest than that of the shareholders (the principal). Rather than a principal/agent problem we get a principal/principal problem. Too many CEOs become major stockholders, and they borrow extensively to get their fix, that the CEO employer ends up guaranteeing loans used by the stock addict to feed his habits is seldom remarked upon until it is too late.

Thus, the CEO becomes dependent on the company and may take actions that are not necessarily objective, but rather in his/her own self-interest (see Salter, 2003).

Evolution

It has been noted by many that the brain-driven organization is today a reality, with the key asset being the people who are working in the organization. Traditionally, the question of knowledge management and organizational learning has been seen in terms of what this means for the organization, both from the CEO's stakeholder management point of view, as well as from the board's governance point of view. Careers have been managed from an organizational-need perspective. Now we may be seeing an inversion of this: individual careers may more and more drive the shaping of the organization, in the sense that executives will now decide for themselves more and more what types of job assignments they are prepared to hold, in terms of what would enhance their own personal and professional development. It is perhaps no longer the board and the shareholders that hold ultimate power, nor the CEO himself, but rather the key knowledge holders/talent holders within the organization. This group will now increasingly be key stakeholders, and thus may play a more important role both as a stakeholder group as well as from a governance point of view. So, the governance equation may indeed be different in the brain-driven, flat, networked organization of the future!

Conclusion

This brings us back to the central theme of the role and responsibilities of the CEO relative to the board. They must be laid out uncritically and without any side-issues in mind, to secure the success of the firm. Or put another way, to be in line with what are the key decisions for success that the firm must tackle. This is what should shape the CEO's agenda. This is what the CEO must be able to focus on and to deliver vis-à-vis both the board and the corporation as a whole.

7

Performance Evaluation of Corporate Boards and Boards of Directors

Fred Neubauer and Helga Krapf

In light of recent global economic developments, top management in big national and international companies has come under heavy criticism. The question has been raised, among others, whether it would be possible or even desirable to evaluate the top management of large international firms, especially the board and supervisory boards, regularly and systematically. This chapter looks at these questions from both an Anglo-Saxon and a Northern European point of view.

Approaches rooted in Anglo-Saxon thinking and experiences

Practically everybody in the hierarchy of a corporation undergoes regular evaluation by a superior. Not only the people on the shop floor of the company, but also the CEO and his lieutenants are subjected to such a review. In most companies, however, board members are exempt from appraisal. More and more practitioners and researchers are finding this situation unsatisfactory.[1] As the pressure to improve board performance grows, the number of board members willing to entertain the idea of such an assessment, even among those who have for years looked askance at performance reviews, seems to be increasing. A widely acknowledged OECD report on corporate governance and many of the codes of conduct for boards that have sprung up in many countries over the last decade recommend such a review.[2] Subjecting a board to any kind of assessment is no triviality. That is why it is prudent to be sure that the reasons for embarking on a board evaluation – breaking with the past – are, indeed, compelling. Further, as very little practical experience exists, many boards, even if they decided to carry out such a review, would not know how.

Why evaluate a board?

Recent, spectacular business collapses share one major commonality. When the reasons for the failures were debated, one central organ was often put to the pillory: the board of directors. The underlying trends here are the increasing accountability of boards, in general, and more specifically, the value of a formal evaluation of board performance from a corporate governance point of view in holding boards accountable.

Any discussion of board evaluation on the international plane immediately raises a question: 'What type of board are we talking about?' The Anglo-Saxon one-tier board (typically composed of executive and non-executive board members)? Or the supervisory board in a continental two-tier system, where the top organization consists of a board of management that runs the company day to day and the supervisory board which is, in principle, composed only of outsiders? The evaluation schemes discussed in this chapter have been heavily influenced by Anglo-Saxon board practices. In a typical Anglo-Saxon board evaluation scheme, non-executive and executive board members are evaluated jointly, but the latter group's performance is judged only from the corporate governance perspective. Managerial performance is evaluated separately. The idea that applying well thought-out assessment processes to supervisory boards can be meaningful seems to be shared by the German Commission on Corporate Governance. Under the leadership of Theodor Baums, that same group recommended, among other procedures, this very approach. However, they left it to the subsequent committee under Gerhard Cromme to formulate requirements for the self-evaluation of boards.[3] The German Corporate Governance Code contains under provision 5.6, 'Examination of Efficiency', the requirement that 'the Supervisory Board shall examine the efficiency of its activities on a regular basis'.[4] At this stage of the discussion, the details of how to go about such a process are still missing.

With very rare exceptions (Japanese boards, for example), in all countries with free market economies boards in publicly quoted companies play a key role in a modern corporate governance system, regardless of the details of the legal framework (one-tier or two-tier board systems). This is the overriding reason for scrutinizing their performance formally and regularly. Unfortunately, until relatively recently, there were few tools for conducting such assessments in a formal way.

Suggestions for filling this void have come out of several corners. They can be grouped in two categories, according to who applies them. The first group comprises the evaluation schemes outsiders apply. The second group includes schemes the companies themselves use. Among the schemes outsiders apply are the efforts of business journals like *Business Week* and *Fortune*. Both publish annual lists of America's 'best' and 'worst' boards, which are based on the opinions of institutional investors, corporate governance experts, investor advisory firms, or shareholder-rights activists, to name the more important ones.[5] The second category, schemes that are administered internally (a self-evaluation of the board for instance), will be discussed here.

Before going into detail, a word of caution. Despite the considerable recent progress in this field, these approaches are still at an early stage of development. This should, however, not distract from the fact that these schemes have, in the eyes of those who have been subjected to them, in most cases produced meaningful results. They have, at any rate, produced at least two important results. Many boards are now aware, or more aware, of major 'issues' in their performance. These schemes have also provided a 'first-cut' platform from which to look at that issue systematically.

How to evaluate whom?

In principle, at the top of an organization several types of internal evaluation are conceivable, depending on which part of the top organization is to be scrutinized. Here are the most obvious:

- Evaluation of the board as a group,
- Evaluation of individual board members, and
- Evaluation of the chairman of the board.

The popularity of these evaluations varies. The percentage of companies who subject *their board as a group* to a formal evaluation is growing steadily, and it seems that at least in the US almost every second company conducts such an assessment. According to the Korn/Ferry 28th Annual Board Director Study of Fortune-listed companies, almost half the sampled companies claim to carry out such an evaluation (see Table 7.1). According to another study, SpencerStuart's board index of S&P 500 companies, the percentage is even higher: 67% of the sample evaluate the board as a group.[6] In contrast, only a relatively small percentage of companies conduct *an evaluation of individual board members*. In the Korn/Ferry study the figure hovered around 20% during the last three years for which data is available. What might explain this reluctance to scrutinize individual board members?

One possible explanation is that assessing the performance of a group is far less threatening than assessing individuals. When the group is the focal point the individual enjoys the protection of the 'herd'. The individual board member standing in the limelight is likely to feel more threatened.

Table 7.1   Observed evaluation practices

	1999	2000	2001
Evaluation of entire board	37%	40%	42%
Evaluation of individual directors	20%	19%	19%
Evaluation of the CEO	56%	64%	67%

Source: Korn/Ferry International, 2001, pp. 5–6

One school of thought suggests that assessment centred on individual performance could have an undesirable by-product: the collegiality and mutual trust so necessary on a board can be easily damaged or even destroyed. As we will show in the discussion of practical evaluation systems below, this danger can be controlled with a carefully thought-through process. Naivety is misplaced in this context – everybody around the board table has an opinion on everybody else. Why should mature board members not put these opinions on the table for open discussion? This way of thinking seems to be gaining acceptance in more and more companies – at least as a concept. As the Korn/Ferry analysis shows, 71% of the respondents believe that the performance of individual directors *should be* regularly evaluated.[7]

In this chapter, we will not only restrict ourselves to discussing internally administered evaluation systems, we will also concentrate on the evaluation of individual board members. We have two reasons for our choice. The evaluation of individual board members has so far drawn limited attention from both practitioners and academic researchers. It is largely virgin territory and, as such, a particularly attractive investigation. Second, although the calibre of the individual contribution may not correlate directly with the overall success of a board, it is a major contributor to it. Readers who are interested in the other types of evaluations mentioned above should refer to the Further Readings section at the end of this chapter.

Evaluation of individual board members

In conducting an assessment of the performance of individual board members, companies typically apply one of two approaches. Either *everybody* on the board is asked to assess the performance of every other board member (peer review by the whole board) or *a small, carefully selected group of board members* is asked to conduct the assessment (review by committee).

A process involving the whole board in the assessment

The authors have been involved in developing such evaluation procedures in several large companies. During this work it has become clear that the procedure requires considerable sensitivity. One reason for using the right dose of sensitiveness or *Fingerspitzengefühl* is that the role of a board member (which can be one reference point for the evaluation) is anything but sharply defined. Experienced board members are nevertheless in a position to form an opinion on the performance of a peer. As the old example goes: people who are experienced in the field are in a good position to judge whether somebody speaks a foreign language well, even if they cannot articulate their exact reasons, or benchmarks. The same holds true for board performance. Becoming aware of the lack of such benchmarks can be a good reason for a board to give some thought to the matter. As William George, Professor at IMD and until May 2002 Chairman of the Minneapolis-based medical technology company Medtronic, suggested in a recent interview with the *Harvard Business Review*, every board should establish a corporate governance committee.[8] Its task is to draft principles of corporate governance. Among other things these principles should spell out job descriptions of the parties involved in the internal governance of the corporation.

Another difficulty in judging the quality of the contribution a board member makes is the fact that, at the board level, many decisions are judgement calls in which intuition plays a major role; in such cases it is virtually impossible to judge whether the decision process has been flawed. Regardless, a group of experienced peers can still judge whether a board member's judgement has been persistently right or only rarely, an important finding.

All these intricacies suggest two things. In this delicate process, the chairman has an important role, and the degree of formality must be limited. Nevertheless, our practical work has shown that a certain amount of structure helps. Such a structure appears below. The suggested approach is obviously not meant as a straitjacket, but rather as food for thought to help boards to find their own solution.

Figure 7.1 presents an overview of the key steps necessary to conducting such a process. The model stemmed both from our practical work with boards of international companies and with our observations of other practitioners' methods. Some conceptual thinking on the subject has informed our approach. Since the evaluation of individual directors is neither widespread nor well established, it should be no surprise that at this early stage a rigorous conceptual framework is still missing. However, the description of practices observed lends a certain freshness to the discussion and increases its credibility in the eyes of practitioners who are typically inclined to ask what other companies have done with respect to board evaluations. In this case the authors follow a predominantly pragmatic Anglo-Saxon tradition in which one first describes and studies successful practices and then comes up with an overarching framework.

Step 1: Identification of desirable attributes

The starting point in creating an assessment scheme is to identify the desirable attributes in an 'acceptable director'. Here the whole board should

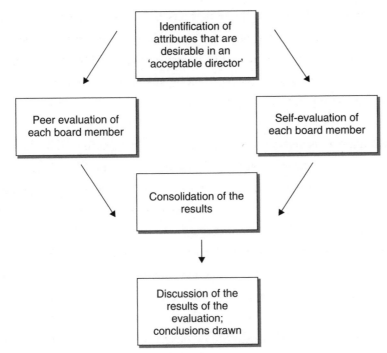

Figure 7.1   Steps in the peer evaluation process

be involved, for two reasons. First, very few boards ever formally raise the question of what is really expected of them. Although general ideas on this matter exist, they have rarely been examined systematically or accepted formally. Entering a board evaluation process may trigger such an assessment. Second, buy-in is achieved only when everybody is invited to present their ideas and formulate the attributes of an acceptable director. In the end, it is important to get broad agreement on the parameters. Once a common ground has been established, a board member will hardly be able to blame a bad selection of criteria if, in his case, the evaluation comes out unfavourably.

Going through this step at the outset has the advantage that, in choosing the characteristics, the company's stage of development can be taken into consideration. After all, it is highly probable that the desirable qualities of a board member in a young start-up company will differ from those of the director of a company at cruising speed.

To stimulate a discussion on criteria, it may be helpful to feed in the thinking of others who have wrestled with the issue. Lee and Plan,[9] whose work can be mentioned here *as pars pro toto*, defined the generic competencies of a director as strategic perspective, business sense, planning and organization, analysis and judgement, managing staff, persuasiveness, assertiveness and decisiveness, interpersonal sensitivity, communication, resilience and adaptability, energy and initiative, achievement motivation. Another source of input may be a list of criteria that practitioners in other companies have already developed (see below). These practitioners were guided by the principle that the attributes should be observable by board members in the course of their board work. One such catalogue of criteria was developed by a European bank, a company 'at cruising speed'. Note that the board had some reluctance about embarking on the process and applying the criteria. Once the process had been carried out, however, the participants viewed the outcome as highly positive. As a company gains experience with the tool, it may refine the list of criteria. The number of criteria, though, should not go beyond roughly a dozen. Too large a list tends to blur the picture rather than add transparency.

Criteria selected by the board of the European bank:
- He/she has a good knowledge of the business, its organization and culture.

- He/she has a good insight into the industries in which the company is active.
- He/she consistently displays a solid commitment to his/her role as board member (for example, prepares well for each board meeting).
- He/she uses his/her knowledge and experience to give the board and management new, strong ideas (distinctive contribution).
- He/she willingly makes his/her contacts to other companies, government agencies or institutions available to the firm.
- He/she expresses concerns and opinions honestly and listens to others' opinions.
- His/her participation on the board enhances team performance and development.
- His/her participation on the board is not restricted by conflicts of interest.
- His/her contribution to the discussions enhances the quality of decisions made by the board, and adds dynamism to the value-creation process of the firm (additive contribution).
- He/she consistently displays solid judgement.

By concentrating on the performance of individual board members, certain aspects normally considered important in a board discussion are deliberately left off this list. A typical example: an assessment of the group dynamics prevailing on the board. Criteria of this nature are by no means ignored; they are covered in the context of the evaluation of the board as a group, which is typically part of an overall evaluation process. As mentioned above, the authors have no intention of discussing the evaluation of the board as a group here; it may suffice to refer to Appendix 1, a catalogue of criteria Campbell Soup developed for such purposes.

Step 2: Peer evaluation

Step two in the evaluation process is peer evaluation. The starting point for peer evaluation is to cast the key attributes identified in Step 1 in a simple questionnaire (refer to Appendix 2 for a sample questionnaire). Every board member fills in such a questionnaire for everybody else on the board. They evaluate their peer board members in two ways: on a numerical scale from one to five (1 = Strongly disagree, 5 = Strongly agree) and through written comments after each criterion. In our experience the latter is more important than the numerical rating as it brings out more subtle points than can be captured numerically. As far as the scale is concerned, some companies have found that the evaluating board members tend to go for the neutral middle ground (i.e. they give in to the temptation to predominantly mark '3' for each criterion). To encourage a clear preference for agreement or disagreement in some companies, the board members are therefore explicitly asked to show a clear preference by not circling the neutral '3'. The practice is disputed.

Completing the questionnaire in a way that makes it useful in the subsequent steps requires a good deal of discipline. It takes time to fill in the questionnaire carefully; each board member must be objective and rigorous. The latter is especially difficult if a board has worked together for a long time and developed a club atmosphere where the urge for harmony outstrips the appetite for an exacting evaluation of a board colleague's performance. This is particularly common in boards of family-controlled enterprises. Some form of guideline for the process has proved to be valuable in practice. In the family-business context, a facilitator could, for instance, ask: 'How would you rate your colleague if he/she was a member of the board of a first-class, publicly owned company?' at the beginning of the questionnaire.

In our experience this approach usually creates a certain amount of healthy distance between a board member and his or her peers, which favours objectivity.

For obvious reasons the name of the appraised as well as the appraising board member needs to appear on the questionnaire. In some cultures, this inclusion may create discomfort, especially when the evaluation is carried out for the first time, when nobody really knows how the information will be used. Confidentiality is, in our experience, paramount. If confidentiality is not assured, the evaluators may not voice their honest opinions of their peers, in which case, the evaluation exercise will generate a bright picture that does not reflect reality. One way to demonstrate a reasonable degree of confidentiality is to engage a trusted third party from outside the firm who serves as a guardian of the data submitted. As the sole recipient of the original data, the outsider can use the completed questionnaires to prepare a dossier for each board member. We will return to the third party's role in more detail in Step 4 below.

Step 3: Self-evaluation

Next comes a self-evaluation by each board member, an opportunity for board members to critically review their own contribution to the board. The same questionnaire as for the peer evaluation is used, but the impersonal 'he/she' will obviously have to be changed to 'I' in every question. Including this step in the process is, in the first place, a matter of fairness. A board member may have good reasons – unknown to the others – for behaving one way or another on the board, and he or she deserves an opportunity to explain them. The additional information may enrich the ensuing discussion of the board member with the chairman on the outcome of the evaluation. In addition, it may be quite revealing to compare the compilation of the opinions of the peers with the self-evaluation.

Step 4: Consolidation of the results

In this phase, the above-mentioned outsider can play a valuable role. To prevent the questionnaires from ending up on the desks of unauthorized people, board members return the filled in questionnaires not to the company, but directly to the go-between. That person compiles the answers, both quantitative and qualitative (verbal), in such way that none of the remarks can be traced to the source. In the end, the result will be one dossier for each board member containing the consolidated answers of the other board members and the self-evaluation. Obviously, the go-between refrains from commenting on the outcome of the individual evaluations, and reports to the chairman any inappropriate use of the process.

The result of the process is, of course, not an objective evaluation of the performance of a board member. The assessment is, nevertheless, based not just on one opinion, the chairman's, but on a whole group of reasonable, responsible peers. This facilitates the discussion of these results between the chairman and the board member – a conversation that is the subject of the next step. One copy of this dossier goes to the person evaluated and the second one to the chairman.

Step 5: Discussion of the results of the evaluation; conclusions drawn

This step is obviously the most delicate part of the process. The discussion of the outcome cannot be conducted in front of the full board. Such a session could all too easily turn into a tribunal, with hardened positions on both sides whenever criticism comes up. This danger is particularly strong when the process is conducted the first time. Once the board members have had some experience, they may be able to discuss the outcome openly around the board table.

The meetings between the chairman and the individual board members are obviously confidential. The chairman should make it clear at the outset that the spirit of the meeting is 'to make good better', to improve the performance of a board member and thus strengthen the board. Recognition should be given to successful contributions. Where weaknesses have been spotted, the chairman and the board member discuss their validity and look into ways to eliminate them. To give an example, in one case where the board of a bank went through the process, one very influential industrialist on the board (a non-executive board member) was criticized by several of his peers for not making his vast connections available to the bank. In the discussion with the chairman the industrialist admitted that he could have done better in this respect and he promised to make more of his connections in the future – a promise he kept.

If the outcome of the evaluation is strongly negative and if there is little promise that improvements will result from the discussions, the termination of the board membership may have to be considered. The most elegant solution in such case would be to ask the board member not to stand for re-election at the end of his tenure. Only highly extraordinary misbehaviours would warrant the request that a member leave the board immediately. Issues of that gravity would, however, hardly be uncovered in a routine evaluation process.

As noted above, in practically all cases where the authors were involved in conducting such a board review process, the outcome has been judged positive by the participants, an attitude that prevailed even after considerable time had elapsed since the exercise. In some instances the process resulted in remedial course work for an individual board member or an educational effort mounted for the total board.

How often will such a process be carried out? According to SpencerStuart's board index[10] of S&P 500 companies, 48% of the companies who evaluate individual directors do so annually. In our experience, conducting such a process every second or third year is sufficient.

Evaluation by a committee of the board

In addition to involving the whole board in the evaluation process, some companies ask a select group of board members to conduct the evaluation of individual board members. A good example of an evaluation by committee was developed by Medtronic Corporation. The former chairman, William W. George, recently described the Medtronic practice as follows:

> Most board members are uncomfortable with the idea of a peer review [. . .] We have instituted another process which has worked well for us. We have a corporate governance committee composed of all outside directors that is responsible for the governance of the corporation and the board. The chair holder of that committee also chairs the nominating sub-committee composed of three directors and him. Since we have board terms of three years, before a director is nominated to serve another term, his or her performance

is assessed by the sub-committee and a recommendation is made
to the full corporate governance committee [. . .] We did have a
situation [. . .] with a director who was not working out and who
was not asked to stand for re-election.[11]

The pharmaceutical group Novartis in Basel, Switzerland, is going to use
a similar approach. In a recent press release the company announced
that it would establish a corporate governance committee in addition
to the already existing three committees, *Präsidium* (board of directors),
Vergütungsausschuss (compensation committee), and *Prüfungsausschuss*
(review board). The Corporate Governance Committee is responsible both
for appointing new members to the board of directors and evaluating current
members of the board of directors. Board members who are up for re-election
will also undergo an evaluation of their performance by the Corporate
Governance Committee.[12]

Which one of the two approaches is superior: evaluation by the whole board or
evaluation by committee? There is too little tangible evidence to say. It may
therefore be advisable to suggest to companies that are novices in this area
or where the culture does not *a priori* favour the evaluation of board member
performance, to take the committee approach when they first introduce the
process. They can always switch to a review by the full board later on.

Concluding remarks

Today, the accountability of boards in the public eye is by far greater
than it was only a decade ago. In the past, directors rarely faced serious

consequences for corporate failure. In the first nine months of fiscal year 2002, the US Securities & Exchange Commission asked federal courts to bar 71 directors from ever serving on a public company board again (in contrast to 51 requests in 2001) to name just one example of this development.[13] Furthermore, if the growing number of lawsuits is any indication, there are good chances that this development has not yet come to an end. According to the Class Action Clearing House of the Stanford Law School, the number of class action suits against companies and directors for alleged securities fraud has grown in the US from roughly 100 in 1996 to almost 500 in 2001.

One way to restore some of the lost public trust in the functioning of the board would be to produce credible evidence on the part of the boards for their efforts to continuously improve their performance. The regularly recurring assessment of the performance of boards (as well as the proof that the company has freed itself from poor performers at that level) can contribute to this development.

Further Reading

Bernhardt, W. (2000) 'Qualitätsmessung für den Aufsichtsrat', *Frankfurter Allgemeine Zeitung*, No. 169, 24 July 2000: 27.

Charan, R. (1998) *Boards at Work: How Corporate Boards Create Competitive Advantage*, San Francisco: Jossey-Bass.

Conger, J.A., D. Finegold, and E.E. Lawler (1998) 'Appraising Boardroom Performance', *Harvard Business Review*, Vol. 76, Iss. 1: 136–148.

Ingley, C. and N. van der Walt (2002) 'Board Dynamics and the Politics of Appraisal', *Corporate Governance: An International Review*, Vol. 10, No. 3: 163–174.

Neubauer, F. (1997) 'Evaluating the Chairman: No Longer a Taboo', *Perspectives for Managers*, Vol. 38, Iss. 10, Lausanne: IMD.

Appendix 1: Campbell Soup company board standards

In May 1995 Campbell's board governance committee instigated a new process for evaluating its board's performance and effectiveness. As a first step, all directors completed a board evaluation questionnaire. Each director rated from 1 to 5 (and, in most cases, provided written comments) each of the following 15 standards:

1. The board knows and understands the company's vision, strategic precepts, strategic plan and operating plan.
2. The board reflects its understanding of the company's vision, strategic precepts, strategic plan and operating plan in its discussions and actions on key issues throughout the year.
3. Board meetings are conducted in a manner that ensures open communication, meaningful participation and timely resolution of issues.
4. Advance board materials contain the right kind of information.
5. Board members receive their materials sufficiently in advance of meetings.
6. Board members are diligent in preparing for meetings.
7. The board reviews and adopts an annual operating budget and regularly monitors performance against it throughout the year.
8. The board regularly monitors the company's income statement, balance sheet and cash flow.
9. The board reviews and adopts an annual capital budget and receives regular written or oral reports of performance against it throughout the year.

10. In tracking company performance, the board regularly considers the performance of peer companies.

11. The board regularly reviews the performance of the CEO.

12. The board and/or the compensation/organisation committee regularly reviews the performance and ethics of the senior officers.

13. The correlation between executive pay and company performance is regularly considered by the board and/or the compensation committee.

14. The board reviews succession plans for the CEO and senior management.

15. The trigger level for board or committee involvement in major business policies and decisions is appropriate.

Source: Neubauer and Lank (1998, pp. 128–129).

Appendix 2: Peer appraisal questionnaire

Confidential

Peer Appraisal

Name of the appraising board member

_____

Name of the board member appraised

_____

Please indicate your view as to the following statements by circling the appropriate number on the 1–5 scale (where 1 = Strongly disagree and 5 = Strongly agree).

To allow for the degree of subtlety appropriate for an evaluation process of this kind, space for verbal comments is provided after each statement. You are encouraged to use it to express the nuances of your assessment.

1. He/she has a good knowledge of the business, its organization and culture.

1 2 3 4 5

Comments:

. . . .

. . . .

2. He/she has a good insight into the business in which our company is active.

1 2 3 4 5

Comments:

. . . .

. . . .

3. He/she is well informed on current economic/political/social issues in our main market(s).

1 2 3 4 5

Comments:

. . . .

. . . .

4. He/she consistently displays a solid commitment to the role of a board member (e.g. is well prepared for board meetings).

1   2   3   4   5

Comments:

. . . .

. . . .

5. He/she uses his/her knowledge and experience to give the board and management new impulses (contributes a creative perspective to the work of the board).

1   2   3   4   5

Comments:

. . . .

. . . .

6. He/she expresses concerns and opinions honestly.

1   2   3   4   5

Comments:

. . . .

. . . .

7. His/her participation on the board enhances team development and team performance.

1   2   3   4   5

Comments:

. . . .

. . . .

8. He/she listens to others' views.

1   2   3   4   5

Comments:

. . . .

. . . .

9. He/she gets to the heart of issues in discussions.

1   2   3   4   5

Comments:

. . . .

. . . .

10. His/her participation on the board is not restricted by conflict of interest considerations.

1   2   3   4   5

Comments:

. . . .

. . . .

11. His/her contribution to the discussions enhances the quality of decisions made by the board. Contributions are constructive and helpful.

1 2 3 4 5

Comments:

. . . .
. . . .

12. He/she helps to manage conflict or disagreement constructively.

1 2 3 4 5

Comments:

. . . .
. . . .

13. He/she stands up for own views against pressure from others.

1 2 3 4 5

Comments:

. . . .
. . . .

14. In general, he/she displays persistently solid judgement.

1 2 3 4 5

Comments:

. . . .
. . . .

15. In general, he/she displays genuine engagement with respect to his/her role as board member (attitude – willing 'to go the extra mile'; regular attendance – not too many other board seats; etc.)

1   2   3   4   5

Comments:

. . . .

. . . .

8
How Governing Family Businesses is Different

John Ward

Family businesses are fundamentally different in corporate governance from widely held public companies. This difference derives primarily from the discrete nature of their ownership. Family ownership concentrates control and allows greater agency in governance. The family can play many roles across the business system, often facilitating and simplifying decision-making processes. This can both lower the costs of governance and enable unconventional, but strategically advantageous, decisions. In addition, the governance practices of family businesses often evolve, reflecting the stages of development in the business and the family. This need to adapt governance over time is both an opportunity and a challenge of family business. Renewing effective ownership agency at different stages in family business development is one of the keys to sustaining the family business advantage in performance.

The nature of family ownership

Family ownership groups are distinct in many important ways. They not only concentrate control, but they often have a strong emotional attachment to their business. Their stake in the business goes beyond economics, and often becomes a source of self-identity and pride. Families can have a sense of moral obligation to other stakeholders, or even view their business as a vehicle for making a positive contribution to society. Family owners often see their business as a social legacy built by past generations, and their sense of mission often includes a desire for this legacy to continue in succeeding generations. Indeed, it is family ownership's combination of a long-term mission and a desire to enable continuity across generations that makes decision making in family businesses so different.

Family ownership is distinct in another important way: it is often a captive economic interest. The lack of readily available liquidity is an important difference between public and family ownership. Often, exiting ownership of family companies is difficult. Some families create legal restrictions on the sale of stock, and many are privately held. In these circumstances, making a market for the sale of stock can be complex. Valuation discounting can complicate questions of pricing, and many transactions are impacted by their tax treatment in transfer. Often, taxation issues make holding an investment in the family company a better economic option, so long as it achieves a certain threshold of performance.

Owning stock in a family company tends to concentrate the wealth of individuals in a single asset. In family ownership groups, a disproportionate percentage of the net worth of many individuals is often tied up in the family business. This means that family business owners, as a group of investors, have less diversification and higher risk than they would as investors in the broader stock market. This concentrated risk makes family business owners more attentive to their investment and tends to keep them more active and engaged.

The combination of concentrated economic and emotional investment is the key difference found in family business ownership. The security of family owners, both emotionally and economically, is often closely tied to the fate of their business. This makes families more committed to fixing what is wrong with their businesses, rather than fleeing them economically. At times, concern for the family's reputation can seem as important as safeguarding the collective family business investment. This combined emotional and economic ethic is often reflected in the family's traditional business values. The continuity of these discrete family business values is what enables family ownership groups to effectively engage their businesses over time through evolving governance practice.

Business governance in public companies

Governance in the public market is built on a paradigm that relates directly to the nature of widely held ownership. Ownership in the stock market votes with its feet, selling when performance is below expectations. The individual shareholders of widely held public companies have little recourse to effect the decisions of their boards or managers. Instead, they join other individuals in the market and create pressure for performance through their collective short-term decisions to buy or sell stock. The governance of public companies reflects this paradigm of inactive but mobile shareholders creating market pressures for performance.

Public companies have independent boards that act primarily as fiduciaries of potentially mobile shareholder interests. These boards operate under the paradigm of maximizing near-term share value in order to sustain and grow their pool of shareholders. Market demand for the company stock is the measure of success, and this market fluctuates daily based on the fluid relationship of many economic factors, both inside and outside of the company. Because of this, the board of directors is the locus of power in the governance of public companies. The board is charged with the oversight of management, and must assure that management is creating value that will be recognized in the market.

In widely held public companies, management is often perceived as self-interested. Active governance is seen as necessary to curbing management abuses, as well as assuring the effective alignment of management interests with ownership interest. The boards of these public companies spend a great deal of time and effort designing systems to control and monitor management activities and compensation, reinforcing a potentially adversarial relationship. In addition, boards and their practices are under increasing scrutiny today, and many new laws and regulations are being written to reform the governance of public companies. Many of these laws are designed to strengthen the independence of boards and increase their accountability.

As the boards of public companies become more independent and powerful, the expectation that they should provide more than oversight increases, as does the expectation that they should actively direct management on behalf of ownership interests. However, boards focused on corporate performance and share value can become averse to taking risks that may have significant short-term impacts. They can become captive to the conventional wisdom of the market, and forgo more unconventional strategies that might better capture long-term value in their unique market segment. Often, management is better positioned to see how dynamic, new strategies will create value for customers, and improve business performance. Unfortunately, the governance paradigm of public companies does not always enable the pursuit of creative new business strategies.

How governance differs in family companies

Family business governance systems are more uniquely suited to the pursuit of unconventional strategies. Because of the characteristics of their ownership, family businesses can more readily by-pass the adversarial qualities of conventional business governance. Ownership can exert influence and care on multiple levels, making the family an agent of more effective decision making in management, on the board and among owners. Rather than functioning as a costly system of checks and balances, governance in family firms often serves to enable transparency and partnership across the system. This, in turn, can enable the pursuit of strategies that are potentially more productive in the long term, despite short-term costs or risks.

Conventional business governance often focuses on establishing boundaries and defining the separation of decision-making powers. In contrast, family business governance is often focused on establishing productive, procedural engagement across the system. Practices that provide for simultaneous consultations among owners, directors and managers are both cross-fertilizing and enabling of business decisions. Active processes providing for engagement across the system assure an ongoing alignment of interests and objectives over time. In this way, family business governance systems often provide more effective agency for decision making. Rather than struggling over checks and balances, all parts of the system are focused on creating value together.

The active participation of ownership is the key to effective family business governance. Family ownership defines the values, vision and objectives of the business. It articulates the financial goals and performance expectations that guide board and management decisions. Ownership also provides an overall vision of the company, which generally defines the strategic parameters of the business. This clarifies and focuses objectives across the system, and helps set appropriate strategic constraints on board and management decisions. The active engagement of owners is what enables the more effective alignment of decision making in family business.

But good family business governance requires more than the participation of active owners. As in other businesses, the board and management have important functions to fulfil, and well-designed practices are essential. Building clear, shared understanding of the separate functions of the ownership, board and management is an important part of effective family business governance. All the more so because family members often wear multiple hats, functioning as owners, directors and managers. In this situation, clarity of governance functions and roles is often vital to enabling the effective functioning of the system.

While the direct involvement of the family on multiple levels complicates the system, it also provides an important link among the different areas of governance. This built-in link, combined with a positive development of family ties and relationships, can fundamentally change the dynamic of trust that pervades the governance system. A well-functioning system helps build trust within the family, and a good family dynamic in turn becomes an asset to the business. A positive family dynamic enables each separate piece of governance to function better and add more value, while remaining aligned with the other components of the governance system. This spiral of trust is an important factor in facilitating effective business decisions. It is also the chief source of the governance agency advantages found in family businesses.

The stages of family business development

No discussion of governance would be complete without a close look at the patterns of development commonly found in family business evolution. Most family businesses begin with an entrepreneurial founder. Initially, the founder embodies the governance system, being the all-powerful owner and operator of the business. Founders sometimes make use of advisory boards, but they generally retain all decision rights. In many cases, the chief challenge of founders is deciding how to sustain their family business through succession. Passing the business on to the next generation is the great challenge of family companies. Some founders seek a single heir, who can recreate the concentrated power of the owner–operator. More, however, see ownership as a collective economic inheritance of their family, and divide ownership of the business among the members of the family.

When ownership passes down across generations, it passes through distinct stages. The first stage is the sibling or family partnership. This stage often begins with parents sharing ownership with their children. Eventually, the involvement of the parents ends, and the siblings come to share ownership in a partnership spirit. They must decide among themselves how to govern the business, and often this is described as the 'kitchen table' period. The siblings can sit down together and consult informally, and sometimes they form a board to help build consensus for strategy. Often, roles begin to separate at this stage, as some siblings may be active in the business while others are not. From this point on, the level of trust in the family often determines how formal governance practice becomes.

The third generation succession often involves a diverse group of cousins. This generally changes the scale of the family, and differentiates family roles further. Family members may continue to be involved in management, the board and ownership. Ownership holdings can become increasingly variable in size, with some remaining quite concentrated. Family members can be active to varying degrees in the business and governance, and their level of involvement may not necessarily reflect their level of economic interest. These complications generally lead to the development of more formal governance practice. When majority ownership moves outside of management, the board will often take on more of a fiduciary characteristic.

The extent that trust is cultivated directly between the controlling owners and the leaders of management often determines how formal governance practice becomes at this stage, and whether the family can continue to create effective agency in governance.

The next family succession causes another significant change in ownership scale, and often brings to an end the concentration of interests that allowed individual owners to create agency. At this stage, the development of family governance, which functions in parallel to business governance, is often an added feature of an increasingly formal and complex governance system. Effective family governance can continue to enable agency even in widely dispersed family ownership groups. This is particularly true when family members continue to be involved across the governance system, linking ownership, the board, and management. Often, the business at this stage has become a holding company, creating the need for a board that can strategically manage a portfolio of businesses.

The evolution of family business governance

Changes in family scale are a common driver of governance evolution in family companies, as are changes in business scale. As a business grows, it becomes increasingly complex, creating its own demands for a more formal organizational structure. While adapting governance practice to the emerging needs of families and businesses as they grow is a very complex and challenging endeavour, over time it is also unavoidable. Success drives the need to adapt and change. At certain stages, business or family growth will tend to become exponential. All family businesses eventually face this reality. Their ability to respond to these challenges is tested again and again, with each change in scale of the business or the family.

Because family and business life cycles often challenge the effectiveness of existing governance practices, family businesses are actually quite attentive to adapting their practices over time. With each generation succession or change in business scale, family companies are often confronted with the need to recreate their business governance. Family business life cycles can lead to fundamental changes in the roles, functions and practices of the governance system. Faced with the dilemmas of change, families frequently study current best business practices. However, rather than simply adopting prescriptive best practices, families tend to adapt practices to their historic business culture, and so renew the effectiveness of their governance agency over time.

Types of owners and governance

Critical to this process are the different types of owners that emerge and how the family adapts governance roles in relation to these ownership types. Here are five different types of owners found in family businesses.

- *Operating owners* work in the business and are responsible for leading management.
- *Governing owners* are employed to lead governance and monitor operations.

- *Active owners* are family members not employed by the business, but who add business value by remaining knowledgeable, engaged and committed.
- *Investing owners* are family members who focus on the financial performance of the company, and may buy, hold or sell their stock.
- *Passive owners* are family members who pay little attention to the company or the return on their investment.

Most family businesses begin with owner–operators. Often, succeeding generations will also have operating owners, as family members continue to lead management. When ownership is dispersed over time, however, the stake of owner–managers declines. Some families deal with this by creating voting control that is separated from beneficial economic interest. Through voting trusts or special voting stock, the concentration of control is retained and passed on to a group of owner–managers and/or governing owners (or their designated fiduciaries). Businesses that develop a strong culture of family management often try to recreate family leadership of management in succeeding generations by concentrating voting control. In these situations, family managers retain more power than their ownership stake represents, and they can continue to provide business agency to the governance system.

Governing owners are family members who do not work in day-to-day management, but who have a direct, professional involvement in the governance. They can be trustees of voting trusts, directors on boards, or heads of family councils and family offices. In contrast to cultures that favour strong family leadership in management, some families find management involvement problematic. In their experience, family members have often abused positions in management or proved ineffective managers. In order to assure the highest professional standards, some families decided to become governing owners, and prohibit family members from employment in operations. In this case, the family's governing owners are paid to oversee a fiduciary governance system. All business practices become performance based and professional. Governing owners in this system add value by assuring pursuit of the highest business standards and by providing strategic agency between ownership and management in the governance system.

These two examples illustrate the extremes at either end of the spectrum. In cases like these, the history of the family often determines whether the family is deeply involved in management or consciously removed from involvement. Families that chose one or the other extreme tend to have had family problems in the past that impacted the business. Sometimes, their businesses have grown quite rapidly, and the family sees itself as either poorly prepared to share ownership control or without a good candidate to direct management of the business. Some families respond to these challenges by creating governance structures that can 'protect' the business from the family. The perceived purpose of these structures is to assure that control is retained in a way that maintains business agency. Often, they also serve to perpetuate the family business by preventing excessive extractions of capital by ownership.

Most family businesses evolve governance roles less dramatically and over a longer period of time. Family successions gradually lead to a broadening spectrum of ownership types. Governance roles evolve in relation to this general shift toward decreasing concentrations of ownership. Many family businesses continue to have both operating and governing owners, often working as a team and also incorporating non-family professionals. This leadership group tends to represent an increasingly smaller ownership interest over time. As the family business matures, choosing individuals to fulfil these leadership roles becomes one of the most important and difficult functions of the governance system. Equally important is creating engagement and commitment with the ever-expanding ownership group. As ownership interests are broadened and diluted, maintaining a coherent ownership culture that remains an asset to the business becomes increasingly important and challenging.

In mature family business systems, controlling ownership is often widely scattered across a large family. With each generational succession, individual shareholders have less intimacy with the business and tend to become more like investors in the stock market. When this happens, governance can increasingly evolve toward the fiduciary public ownership model. In order to retain their unique governance agency, family businesses as this stage must develop family governance that can create a controlling pool of active owners. Family shareholders will naturally become investors or passive owners if they are not engaged in meaningful governance. The development of family governance that is effectively linked to business governance can help transform large, dispersed ownership groups into coherent, active ownership groups. Families that succeed in this effort build in the cultural foundation that enables ongoing governance agency within ownership.

The governance practices of mature family business

The examples above describe different ways that family businesses mature. In addition, some families 'prune' the ownership tree by buying out disinterested branches of the family. Occasionally, one family branch will buy its way back into control. Often, the goal of these processes is to enable the renewal of ownership agency in governance. The more the ownership of a family business becomes dispersed and disinterested, the more it loses its special ability to add value. In addition, large families with mature businesses may increasingly seek to extract capital rather than reinvest it for growth. The family ownership itself, through its economic dependence on the business, can become a drag on the ability of the business to pursue the best strategies for long-term value creation. The fact that some family businesses will expend considerable amounts of their capital to reconsolidate ownership control is a measure of the importance of renewing ownership agency to long-term value creation.

Family business systems can move forward or backward in their evolution. Many become fundamentally unstable because of family or business pressures and are sold or taken public to generate liquidity. Competing demands for capital need to be strategically managed, if family businesses are to achieve long-term continuity. If family ownership does not effectively renew its strategic agency over time, then the system will move increasingly toward a market-driven paradigm or seek to reconsolidate control. Families can follow many different strategies to renew their ownership agency as their business systems mature. An increasing number of mature family businesses are developing family governance practices as part of this effort. They recognize that to renew effective agency in their ever-larger ownership groups, they must engage a vast majority of family shareholders in building a shared vision of the business.

As family businesses mature, both the family and business sides of the system are transformed. Governance faces increasing functional challenges from both sides and must evolve in response to both. One common approach to this dual challenge is to create parallel family and business governance. In this governance model, parallel structures are created for the family and business. The business governance responds to the increasingly rigorous functional needs of the business by pursuing ever-more professional practices and competencies. The family governance responds to the fragmentation of ownership by generating collective processes that can re-engage the family and generate an active voice and vision of ownership. The parallel sides of this governance model are then linked by processes, which enable agency at key points in decision making. Ideally, each side of the system functions well, and the links are strong enough to assure ongoing alignment of governance across the parallel system.

Typically, parallel governance features an increasingly professional business board and a democratic family council, which often develops increasingly formal practice over time. The board of directors, elected by the share-holders, sits at the top of business governance. These boards typically have a family chairperson and include family managers and/or governing owners, as well as a significant number of independent directors. These boards function much like the boards of public companies, providing oversight and direction to management, and acting as fiduciaries of shareholder interests. Family governance is built separately and is usually based on democratic principles. Family cultural practices around issues of branch representation, variable ownership interests, blood versus in-law relations, etc. can all impact the development and evolution of family governance. Practices can be quite variable, ranging from informal gatherings to the development of highly structured and professional institutions like family councils and family offices. As families and the resources they manage grow, so generally does the formality of their governing systems.

The special role of the family business board

Even early in their development, family businesses can benefit from a board of directors. Often, advisory boards can assist founding entrepreneurs achieve the first succession transitions more successfully. Founders are frequently so focused on the development of their business that they do not prepare effectively for succession. A good advisory board can help a founder refocus on the task of creating continuity through transmission. Succession is the single greatest challenge of family businesses at all stages of their development. A good board of directors will help assure that a process for succession is in place and that leadership candidates are being developed well in advance. This can be particularly challenging in family businesses, especially early in their development.

The boards of first and second generation family companies can also play a vital role in transmitting the business knowledge necessary to continue value creation. Founders and their successors often need help consolidating an understanding of the core competencies of their businesses, as well as transmitting this knowledge. Boards can help build management and operational structures that can take the business through the next level of growth. Independent directors can serve to bring significant professional experience to family business boards even in the early stages of development. Business perspectives from outside of the company often provide added insight and creativity.

As family businesses grow, their boards tend to become more and more involved in strategy. The development of strategic planning processes puts the board of directors directly between management and ownership. The board must review the planning processes of management, and assure that the business strategy reflects both the reality of the company's capabilities and the opportunities provided by the economic environment. The board must also assure that this strategy reflects ownership's financial objectives, both in the short and long term. At a higher level, the board must assure that ownership and management share the same strategic vision of the company. The board must understand the aspirations of the family for the business, as well as the competitive capabilities and market potential of the business. If there is misalignment of capabilities and expectations, the board has the special role of fostering communication around these issues and assuring their resolution.

The early use of independent directors can be highly valuable to family business boards. Non-family directors can often induce the family to consider difficult issues that would otherwise be avoided. This enables the family to achieve a more effective level of planning. Succession transitions and the strategic alignment of ownership and management visions are two areas where families often struggle. Another is the allocation of capital. As family businesses grow, they often face difficult choices about how to prioritize capital investments. Multiple family and non-family managers may come before the board and 'compete' for investment capital. The board must assess these decisions rigorously, reviewing their financial and strategic importance. Independent directors can help assure that these decisions are made objectively, without being influenced by family ties or biases. The objectivity of independent directors is an important asset on a family business board. Many families recognize the benefit of empowering their independent directors to help resolve the issues that are most difficult for the family.

As family businesses mature into holding companies, their boards become managers of a portfolio of businesses. The board must develop a portfolio strategy, which identifies both the markets it wants to serve and the financial performance parameters it expects from the companies it owns. The board must assess the performance and potential of its companies and decide whether to grow, harvest, or divest each business unit. When targeted market segments with strong potential are underserved, the board must weigh the possibilities of deploying capital for new ventures, partnerships or acquisitions. These decisions are often difficult in family businesses. Family managers can have a personal stake in existing businesses that make divestiture decisions difficult. Management also tends to be enthusiastic about investing in new ventures, partnerships or acquisitions, and there can be a tendency to 'sell' these decisions. A good board will set financial benchmarks for all these decisions in advance, and set timetables for achieving these benchmarks. Managing new ventures, strategic partnerships, acquisitions and divestitures is an important function of boards in mature family companies.

The role of boards in conflict resolution

In the governance systems of family businesses, many important decision rights rest with the board of directors. When making important decisions, a good board will remain ever vigilant to the impact of these decisions on the family. Many difficult decisions can stress the coherency of the family ownership group or management. Sometimes, boards must work to mitigate conflict, and trusted independent directors can often play a special role in this process. When there are conflicting views about a decision, independent directors can lend their objectivity to both the discussions and the decision-making process. In many cases, an effort must be made to educate the wider family about the issues and to clarify the intended purpose of board actions. Independent directors are sometimes called upon to offer their impartial views and ultimately the board itself becomes the final mediator of some decisions dividing ownership.

When the board acts as final mediator it enables decisions. Family business conflict often leads to indecision, and the authority of the board assures that important business outcomes are achieved in a timely way. Frequently there is little room to compromise and the board must function like a panel of judges making a final judgement. This dynamic can perpetuate conflict if adequate attention is not given to the process of decision making. Family business boards must assure that there is thorough consultation with the family ownership in decision making. Family owners need to be informed, as well as given an opportunity to voice their opinions. When people feel they have been heard, they more readily accept outcomes, even if they are contrary to their views. Creating adequate, ongoing consultation with ownership is one of the key challenges facing family business boards.

This is the main purpose of parallel family and business governance in mature family companies. Parallel governance provides a framework for consultation processes between the board and the family. It supports the sharing of information and the education of the family, as well as providing a mechanism for ownership to be given a voice as decisions are made. Good family business boards will not only support the development of good family governance practice, but they will recognize the future value of this effort to renewing family business agency. As a family ownership group expands and individual holdings shrink, it becomes increasingly important to have a well-designed and functioning structure for educating and consulting with the family. Without this, fragmenting ownership views will move business governance toward the market-oriented paradigm.

The key to family business agency is building trust between management and ownership. At the mature stage of development, family businesses increasingly rely on their board of directors to help build this link. Creating direct, mutual support between owners and managers takes effort and time. Communication must be valued, and the board is often the conduit of information flowing back and forth across the system. A good board will work to enhance mutual understanding, and it will deal directly and openly with issues and conflict. This transparency becomes more important as the family business system gets larger and more complex. For the board to act effectively as final mediator it must be trusted by both management and ownership and it must work openly to foster trust across the system.

Board composition and director selection

Boards have the central governance role in family companies, which makes board composition and director selection processes more critical. Over the course of family business development, governance works best when it aligns board composition with both the development of the type of family ownership and the strategic situation of the business. As controlling ownership moves from operating owners to investing owners over time, the composition and functions of the board will change. Likewise, as a business matures, its strategic situation changes. The board will need to develop new competencies and practices that enable ongoing, rigorous assessment of business strategy over time.

The evolution of board composition can be quite variable in family companies. Most often, this is linked to the level of family ownership involvement in management and the size of the business over time. While management holds a controlling ownership stake, boards tend to be composed of managers, and may or may not include outside directors. Many of the first non-management directors on family business boards are family shareholders representing significant ownership interests found 'outside' of management. The presence of governing owners on boards becomes increasingly common as ownership successions move control out of management. Families that do not have management successors evolve their board composition more quickly, and often include a significant number of independent directors. These directors assist the family in generating effective oversight of their professional managers. Generation succession can shift the types of owners holding controlling interest in the family company over time, and this tends to drive the pace of evolution in board composition. Company size can be another driver in this process. The boards of smaller businesses tend to evolve their composition and practice more slowly, whereas the boards of businesses that grow rapidly must be more responsive to the increasing functional demands of the business.

Choosing directors in family companies can be very complicated and challenging. Many families begin with boards composed entirely of family. Adding non-family directors for the first time can raise many issues, particularly in families with a strong tradition of leading management. In this case, some family members tend to view independent directors as a potential threat to owner–manager agency. As we have seen earlier, independent directors can play vitally important roles on a family business board, and their expertise and objectivity tend to add considerable value to governance at all stages of business development. Many mature family businesses have a significant number of independent directors on their boards, and some have a majority of independent, outside directors.

Family businesses have an opportunity to add considerable value to their governance by carefully selecting the right independent directors. Candidates should be highly experienced, objective and knowledgeable. To assure independence, they should not be drawn from associated businesses, vendors or clients, such as banks or law firms. Active chief executives often make the best independent directors because they bring an understanding of strategic issues, and they know what business criteria should be considered in making board-level decisions. Good independent directors can also bring specific industry knowledge or functional expertise that enhance the competency base of the board. Well-rounded candidates who bring leadership experience can add the most value to a family business board. This is particularly true if they are sensitive to the challenge of governing a family company, and have the interpersonal skills to help build dialogue and understanding.

The conventional wisdom of best practices in public companies is for the board to be composed almost exclusively of independent directors. Often, this is seen as necessary in order to create a balance of power with the CEO. In family companies, this is rarely the case. Most families maintain a significant number of family owner–directors on their boards, and some families maintain a family ownership majority. The selection of family directors is another challenging and highly variable practice in family business governance. Early on, selection is often based on management responsibility or relative ownership interest. The largest shareholders and the leaders of management commonly sit on the boards of young family companies. As long as family managers continue to lead the company, they usually remain on the board and are seen as representing the family as well as management.

Choosing family directors who are not leaders in management becomes more difficult as ownership interests are dispersed. Many families initially pursue representational models based on family branches, but as generations branch further this tends to become cumbersome. Family boards often expand to an inappropriate size when they try to accommodate branch representation in succeeding generations. In addition, branch representation does not reflect governance best practice, which holds that all directors must represent the best interests of all shareholders in their fiduciary capacity. Representation by branch, while a common practice, tends to institutionalize a factional view of the family ownership. Many families have significant historical and cultural branch differences, which are often related to their level of management involvement early in the family business's development. Often, in later generations, governance must adapt to overcome these historical patterns, and create practice that is more consistent across the family.

Ultimately the best family business boards use a competency-based selection process to choose family directors. Family candidates must have a high degree of business knowledge, as well as a thorough understanding of the business itself, including its history and strategy. They must be financially literate, and willing to spend the time necessary to prepare for meetings. Many families look for candidates who have already demonstrated a commitment to both the business and the family, and sometimes a previous active involvement in family governance is a prerequisite. Prospective candidates are often trained over a period of time in business concepts, and their aptitude for learning is assessed. Finally, personal qualities are an important consideration. Are candidates open-minded? Are they good communicators and capable of engaging in board deliberations? Do they exhibit good character and sound judgement? Will they be trusted by other family members, directors and managers?

Adapting governance practice in mature family businesses

Mature family business systems have to respond to the increasingly complex functional demands in both the family and the business. Parallel family and business governance allows the simultaneous pursuit of new practices in both areas. The proper alignment of decisions depends upon clearly delineating roles and processes across the system. Management, the board and the family ownership all have distinct jobs to do, and defining these roles clearly is important. Written policies can help clarify boundaries in governance. Policies can help designate decision rights and also create clarity around decision-making processes in advance.

Management, boards and family governance institutions often develop their own, separate, written policies. This creates the need for consultation processes that enable deliberation and alignment of these policies across the system. The family ownership should be aware of decision-making policies at every level, and these practices should be acceptable to a plurality of ownership. Building clarity of expectations about the roles and processes of governance is critical across the family business system. This clarity is especially important within the family, and can help individual family members better differentiate their roles as managers, directors and owners.

Equally important are fair processes that enable ongoing consultation across the system in decision making. While clarifying decision rights is vital to the system, so is the ability to inform and influence decisions. Each group must be willing to be informed by and consult with the other two in decision making. There must be a commitment to hearing a full articulation of arguments for and against a decision, as well as a willingness to fully explain the final outcome. Family business systems that do not create governance structures and processes that enable consultation and full explanations can ultimately face ongoing conflict over decision rights.

Family business systems frequently need clarity about how governance consultation is triggered and how it will be conducted. This can be vital to enabling decision-making processes to function optimally. Sometimes decisions made easily by one part of the system have unforeseen consequences or effects in another part of the system and end up unexecuted or contested in follow-up deliberations. At other times, the most difficult and complex issues may necessitate coordinated decision-making across multiple levels of the governance system. In both cases, the effectiveness of both major and minor decisions may depend upon an ability to trigger advance consultation and then efficiently conduct consultation processes. Having ready-made processes in place can create clarity about governance practices and build trust across the system. This in turn can help enable more efficient and appropriate decision making without extensive consultation. Many decisions are most effective when they can be made at the right level of the system. When those responsible for a decision have ownership of it, they will also tend to assure its best execution.

Active communication that flows freely across the system is the most critical component of building fair processes for decision making. Good communication builds understanding, flushes out hidden issues, and helps articulate the most important criteria in decision making. Good communication also goes two ways, and involves listening as well as explaining. Fair processes enable decisions. When the governance system is perceived as impartial, consistent and capable of making well-reasoned decisions, it builds trust. The willingness and ability to deliberate across the system is a key measure of this trust component. A breakdown of trust at one level of the system will often impact the entire system, and care must be given to develop fair processes at each level. The most effective family businesses create clarity about roles and processes across their governance system, and they also bring the same high expectations of excellence and fairness to practise at all levels of their governance system.

Organizing the family and ownership

There are many sources for learning about the best practices of business management and boards, but family and ownership practices are not nearly as standardized. Family governance is highly variable and must usually be carefully adapted over time. Organizing the family and establishing ownership practices can be difficult in large families, and often requires ongoing adaptation for over a decade. Families can sometimes establish their governance practices early on, but often they find that changes in the scale of the family create new challenges and a need for new structures. Models for family councils suggest potential structural solutions, but each family group must explore its own culture and create the combination of practices that best expresses its collective values.

The degree of inclusiveness is a key cultural component of family governance. The family must decide who is a family member. Some families exclude in-laws, some require share ownership, and others include any and all descendants and spouses. Representation is another cultural issue families must address in creating family governance. How important is broad representation from all family branches or representation of the different generations of the family? Participation requirements and restrictions can be another consideration in creating family governance. Should family members be required to participate or restricted from governance roles if they fail to participate regularly? What about the participation of family managers and directors in family governance – should their roles be restricted or should they lead in this effort, too? Each individual family has to wrestle with these questions, and craft a governance practice that reflects its culture and values.

Even the most carefully crafted practices will be challenged by the test of time, and most will need revisions and renewal. Family governance can also develop greater and greater complexity, becoming a multi-faceted governance system of its own. It can include professionally run family offices, charitable family foundations, voting trusts, family councils and ownership councils. Each of these layers in family governance can have its own organizing structures and functions, and these, in turn, must be linked and interrelated to one another and to the larger family business governance system. Wealth creation is often the driver for development of these more complex systems of family governance. Helping the family to manage its wealth can become an increasingly important function of family governance, and one that at times can be critical to enabling the ongoing continuity of the entire family business system.

More typically, family governance functions to enable the family to create coherency and consensus in the widely held ownership group. The chief purpose of family governance is to promote the anticipation of issues and to enable deliberation processes that can resolve these issues. Family governance adds value by preparing the family to make decisions in advance and by building a common sense of identity and mission. In large family groups, transmission of business values and ownership vision is a key function of family governance. Educating the family about the business and about family business practices and governance generally is also important. Providing a structure for information flow and education, for planning family meetings, for preparing the next generation, for assuring the family has fun and builds relationships – these are all important functions of family governance.

Fundamentally though, the most important function of family governance is to create and renew itself. Creating a framework that can organize the family to achieve these many functions is challenging and often takes ongoing effort. Building effective family governance that can foster communication and bring the family together to make decisions is difficult but important work to accomplish over time. Establishing family governance takes leadership and an investment of resources.

The funding of family governance and the process for selecting council members and leaders are two challenging issues that must be resolved. Some families establish trusts that distribute income from the company to the family, and a portion of this money is used to fund family governance. Others treat family governance as a shareholder-relations expense of the company. Most family governance is built on a democratic model, where a family council is elected. The family will hold an annual assembly that functions as a meeting of the entire family where a smaller, representative body can be elected. This smaller family council in turn elects its leadership. Some councils are selected, rather than elected, and sometimes leadership is appointed. This is more often the case in other areas of family governance, such as trusts, foundations, and family offices. Voting in family governance can be based on one vote per family member or one vote per share. Sometimes, separate family and ownership councils are constituted in order to better represent both family and ownership interests and to more effectively fulfil their specific functional areas. Election techniques, as well as representation and qualification requirements can vary across the different structures of a family governance system, depending upon the different functions they fulfil.

Participation in family governance can be professional or voluntary. This frequently depends upon the structures and their functions. Many family governance systems incorporate both professionals (non-family and family) and family volunteers. Expenses are usually paid for participants in family governance, and some families will compensate particular positions within the system that require a serious time commitment, such as council and foundation leaders, trustees, etc. Compensation is sometimes based on a board model and uses per-meeting fees, with additional compensation for chairpersons who organize the meetings.

The value added by family governance

Good family governance can add value in many ways. Some of these are abstract and emotional, while others are very tangible and important. Effective family governance generally allows for the creation of family and ownership policies. Creating and updating these policies over time is an extremely important function of family governance. Family policy can help guide decisions in a number of key areas, including family employment and the family's expectations about leadership positions in management. Many families express preferences for family CEOs or chairpersons. These and other policies governing family employment can guide management and board decisions. Family policies sometimes also include codes of conduct, which create expectations for how family members should interact with each other and with the family business system. They can also establish processes for raising issues and resolving family conflict.

Ownership policies are quite important, and have a wide-ranging impact on the entire system. Ownership policies set the guiding principles of business governance, including the composition of the board, and the director selection process. Ownership policies can set financial goals, risk expectations and performance measures for the company. They can also determine appropriate dividend and reinvestment levels, and set out the principles governing shareholder liquidity, including policy regarding share redemptions and company loans. Some ownership groups create formal shareholding agreements that establish rules for share ownership and transference, while others create less formal policies that seek to clarify the standard rights and responsibilities of ownership.

Good family governance recognizes existing family practices, and tries to write them down in clear statements of policy. The articulation and exploration of practices illuminates many issues and gives the ownership family the opportunity to better understand itself and to learn about other trends and practices. Creating policy is forward-looking work. It frames principles for making decisions in the future. Effective governance works within a framework of well-articulated principles. Decision making is the test of this policy framework, and the best governance systems will recognize the ongoing need to adapt policies over time. Written policies that are thought of as fixed are often inappropriate. When policies can be adapted and changed over time, governance remains responsive and forward-looking.

Family governance can add considerable value by actively creating and adapting family and ownership policies over time. This takes ongoing engagement in the family, as well as between the family and its business. This engagement is critical to maintaining family business continuity as the family grows and ownership becomes increasingly dispersed. Families that can continue to work together for their mutual benefit and in support of their businesses can add considerable value. They can come to speak with one voice, in this way building coherent ownership views and family consensus that adds intangible, emotional value. It is the emotional and financial commitment of the family that enables the special agency found in family business, and the creation of this vital, abstract asset is the chief value added of effective family governance.

Summary

Family businesses outperform other businesses. They accomplish this despite being in many different industries and following many different patterns of development. One important factor shared by all family businesses is the discrete quality of their ownership groups, and the agency that this can allow in business governance. Family businesses and their ownership groups go through patterns of evolution in their development, which can impact ownership's interaction with the business. Changing levels of ownership involvement, in management or business governance, has an impact on ownership agency over time. The size of the business and the size of the family also impact agency, and changes in business or family scale can often create the need to renew governance agency.

Effective ownership families adapt to the changing needs of their business and family groups. They recognize the interrelated and symbiotic relationships of the business and family systems, and work to renew the strategic agency they share. Developing and adapting governance practice is the key to enabling the continuity of this strategic agency over time. Well-adapted governance practice becomes increasingly vital as the family and business grow older and larger, and the number of people and resources being managed increases exponentially. This constant need to adapt and change keeps family business systems focused on the future. When combined with a family commitment to continuity and transmission, this can create governance systems that remain more active and responsive, even as they increase in complexity. Families that succeed in building effective governance are often capable of renewing the intangible assets of ownership trust and commitment. These are the key ingredients of agency in the family business system.

Part III

Learning from Past Experience

9

Cobra versus Commerzbank, War at the Helm of Elicore, and National Life

Commented by Bill George

Cobra versus Commerzbank

Commerzbank was the fourth largest bank in Germany in 1999. Its primary customers were the German *Mittelstand*, the small and medium-sized (SMEs) businesses which were mostly family owned or family operated. These SMEs are a critical component of the German economy and Commerzbank was proud of its tradition of financing the vast majority.

The European banking industry in the 1990s was fragmented, with most countries having a large number of small banks, as well as a lack of competition and excessive capacity. According to a PriceWaterhouse report published in 1998,[1] increasing the average size of banks to achieve economies of scale, as well as expanding the product and service offering of banks, would result in gains for the industry which could be passed on to the customers, if barriers to competition become even lower. Banking consolidation was a subject of much discussion in 1999, with the introduction of the euro, increasing globalization and interdependence of financial institutions, advances in information and financial technologies. Consolidation was a concern for many banks, since as a single European market emerged, banks that were large in their countries would be medium sized on the regional scale and small in comparison to global banks. However, differing IT, legal and tax systems made consolidation difficult in practice. Therefore most consolidation that occurred took place domestically.

Commerzbank was too small to compete as a major eurozone bank but too large to do well as a German niche player. As a result, the bank had been a takeover target for years.

In April 2000, an investment group called Cobra revealed a 9.9% stake in Commerzbank, and its intention to increase that stake. Hansgeorg Hofmann, former board member of Dresdner Bank, headed Cobra. Cobra's parent was Rebon, a Dutch holding company owned by Clemens Vedder and Klaus-Peter Schneidewind. Hofmann headed Dresdner's investment banking unit before he was forced to resign in 1997 after admitting to income tax evasion. Vedder and Schneidewind were German billionaires who had a reputation for covertly building up stakes in companies and then selling them at a profit one to two years later. Karl Ehlerding was another member of the Cobra group. Another German billionaire, Ehlerding was the majority shareholder of WCM, an investment and real estate company. WCM was well known as a ruthless asset stripper of companies. WCM and Rebon had partnered previously to buy and profitably sell stakes in the German retailer Spar. Ehlerding held 4.9% of Commerzbank privately, and WCM held 1% in the bank.

Cobra declared that it wanted to sell its investment in Commerzbank at a premium to a bank that would take it over, thus trying to force a hostile takeover. At Commerzbank's annual shareholder meeting on 26 May, Cobra (then with 17% of the shareholders' voting rights) announced that it would 'help the bank to find a strong European partner'. The share price rose to €44 on speculation. Martin Kohlhaussen, CEO of Commerzbank, accused Hofmann of making 'dangerous' comments, raising fears about a break-up and trying to undermine Commerzbank's commercial strategy. Kohlhaussen began merger talks with Dresdner Bank in June 2000. Cobra was against the merger, claiming that a linking with a bank from another European country would create more value for shareholders. The group was reported to be holding out for a share price of €50.

In July, the banking supervisors BAKred (*Bundesaufsichtsamt für das Kredit-wesen*) blocked Cobra's rights to vote with or sell Commerzbank's shares, claiming that Hofmann as Cobra's legal representative was 'unreliable', referring to the tax evasion allegations against Hofmann in 1997. Following the passing of a new German corporate tax law on 14 July allowing companies to sell their non-core holdings and pay no tax on capital gain, Dresdner gained €9 billion in reserves while Commerzbank gained a mere €1.7 billion. So while Dresdner's share price rose to €48, Commerzbank's fell to around €37. Kohlhaussen continued to press for a 53:47 valuation, while Dresdner favoured 60:40. The merger talks collapsed soon after.

In September 2000, Kohlhaussen tried to persuade Generali and Banco Santander Central Hispano SA to double their stakes (currently around 5%). Together with other allied shareholders, this would have given Kohlhaussen a friendly set of shareholders controlling around 22%, thus diluting Cobra's stake and shutting it out. Generali did increase its stake to 10%, but there was no deal with BSCH. Mediobanca increased its holding to 2%. Several shareholder action groups expressed the view that an extraordinary general meeting was needed, for Kohlhaussen to justify his defensive action. The bank rejected calls for an EGM.

In January 2001, Cobra reduced its stake to just under 10%, and BAKred reinstated its voting rights. While some viewed Cobra as a precipitator of change in the German banking industry, others viewed it as destabilizing a fundamental part of the German economy. There was a great deal of anticipation of conflict at the Commerzbank AGM on 25 May 2001. However, Commerzbank held its AGM as planned, with no agenda items from Cobra.

Q: For you, what is the main issue of this case?

A: This case looks at the problems of corporate raiders, who have different objectives than the trustees of the bank. It's clear that Cobra is strictly interested in short-term gains and has no interest in the future of Commerzbank. The bank had a very important role in German business, supporting family-owned business, which is the heart of German industry. Family businesses depend on banks for financing to avoid going to the public market. Typically in family-owned business, the owners have a longer-term view of their success. They look to a bank that understands them and provides them with that long-term support. Commerzbank fulfilled that role. For it to be sold to another bank really undermines the structure of German industry.

Q: What do you think about Cobra and its intentions?

A: The management members of Cobra were criminals. They confessed wrongdoing, they had been forced to resign in the past because of tax fraud, and they were known as being shrewd and ruthless arbitrageurs and were involved in a bribery scandal with the Christian Democratic Union. They didn't want to own the bank; they wanted just enough control to force a sale for short-term gain. Making this very public put an acquisition premium in the stock, because the holders of the stock and the hedge funds saw an opportunity for short-term gain as well. As a result, the stock was inflated. The corporate group expressed their view that the bank was worth $50 a share. Kohlhaussen responded that the value was $38. In fact, it was actually worth even less because of the acquisition premium. It is difficult to try to manage the bank for the long term, rather than succumb to the pressure of the short-term gain of one shareholder.

If you study the case of ABB, it's exactly the same situation: the conflict between the long-term shareholder (Wallenberg family) and the short-term shareholder (Martin Ebner, the bad boy of Swiss industry) put a great deal of pressure in the short term. And you can't run a business that way: you make big mistakes.

Q: How can you prevent that?

This situation can be prevented by having a series of legal strictures which make it very difficult to come in and take over your organization. These strictures range all the way from poison pills to the 'Just say no' defence developed by a lawyer named Martin Lipman. In the end the best defence is good performance. At Medtronic, I worked very hard to avoid this by getting the stock price up through good results, to keep raiders away. That was clearly my motivation in having a good long-term stock position – not an inflated one. I think people are often not willing to take these people on. In this case, Kohlhaussen was willing to fight them. He fought and eventually got Cobra out, to his credit.

Q: You do not seem to believe that every company needs to be big and dominant?

A: No, the whole experience was a tragedy. The only good thing here was that they got Cobra out. Mid-sized banks have a role to play. There is a feeling in the world that if you're not number one or two, you're nothing. That is misreading the situation. Commerzbank has 40% of all the privately held companies in Germany as its customers. They are number one in that segment. That is something that Deutsche Bank cannot take away from them. They don't have to play in the big world of Citicorp and Deutsche Bank and Crédit Suisse. They can play in their own world and be very successful.

Q: What could Commerzbank have done better?

A: Attorneys need to put the legal provisions in place well in advance: (1) to make sure the provisions are in place and (2) to make sure the board are prepared to fend off takeover attempts that would not be the best for the long-term growth of the company. The board needs to be unified and know exactly what it's doing to fight off raids quickly. This can prevent situations like Grand Met manipulating Pillsbury into a sale. An annual review of these provisions is also helpful.

In terms of management, I think Kohlhaussen handled the situation well. It was not in the best interest of the bank and he fought them off. When you say you have to run an organization for the shareholders, you have to be clear about which shareholders: minority shareholders interested in short-term gain, the long-term shareholders that have a commitment, the family members who have their money in it, the customers, or employees who have their pensions tied up in it, the hedge funds who want to see the stock go down. At Medtronic, we managed the company for the patients first, and then the long-term shareholders. If you don't have a long-term interest in the stock, then this is the stock for you. People bought it because they knew it was right. It is important for the board to be committed to the mission and values of the company. Without that commitment you have nothing.

Q: So what do you think of raiders in general?

A: I think corporate raiders are the destruction of industry and laws and rules need to be put in place to prevent them. The problems in corporate governance that started in the US and came to Europe, really emanated from the raiders of the late eighties – that's where we got off track, looking at the short term instead of the long term. If you look at the great American companies who avoided it, they're doing well: Coca-Cola, Johnson & Johnson, Procter & Gamble. The raiders realized they were not an easy attack. They go after the weak ones. In one sense it's good, because it sharpens up the management, in the longer term they never stick around to build the company. They look at corporations as a giant game of Monopoly.

Case study: War at the Helm of Elicore

6 JULY 2002, EDINBURGH, ELICORE HEADQUARTERS. Chairman Lord Winston Heath had just read the long-awaited proposal from a corporate governance consultant. It described a detailed formulation of Elicore's corporate bylaws, the establishment of several committees and the performance evaluation process for the board of management.

Heath immediately sent a copy to Paul Simon, the chief executive officer (CEO), noting that he wanted to send the paper to the whole board before the next meeting. Three hours later Simon called. His voice was as cold as ice:

> I have read your proposal. I still think we are creating too much bureaucracy, but OK, we can discuss the details. But if you push the proposal for my evaluation, I will resign.

He hung up without waiting for Heath's reply. Heath felt trapped. Tensions between Simon and him had been growing ever since he became chairman at the beginning of 2001. His proposal for a new corporate governance structure and Simon's arbitrary decision to change the accounting rules so that Elicore would still show double-digit growth rates had been the latest incidents.

Heath's business instincts told him something was brewing. But the numbers would probably only deliver a clear picture at the end of the year. As he mulled things over, the telephone rang. It was Walter Dale, a member of the board of directors:

> Hello, I am eagerly awaiting the new corporate governance proposals, to be discussed at the upcoming board meeting.

What could Heath do? What should he do?

Corporate governance at Elicore

Elicore was a global manufacturer of ventilation and cooling equipment. The company had been in a turnaround situation when Simon joined as CEO in 1993. Then, only 25% of the company's sales were generated abroad. He had a reputation for being a pushy executive, who got things done. He had grown up in a working-class family and quickly learned that he had to be tough if he wanted to succeed. Previously he had worked for domestic companies, but his lack of international experience was not an issue when he joined Elicore. Simon staged a bloody, but successful, turnaround and drove the company on an accelerated growth path. For more than five years, every quarter had shown double-digit growth in revenue and profits, with major acquisitions along the way. Now 60% of revenue was generated outside the home country and close to 40% of the assets were located abroad. Elicore was one of the UK's top 25 companies.

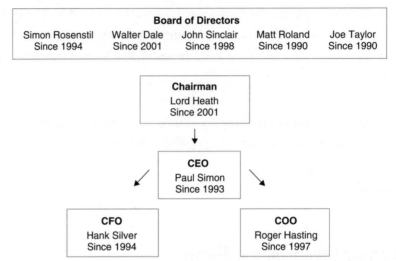

Figure 9.1 Organization of Elicore's corporate governance structure. Source: Steger and Krapf (2002)

Simon shared responsibility for Elicore's day-to-day business with chief financial officer (CFO) Hank Silver and chief operating officer (COO) Roger Hasting. The board of directors, chaired by Heath, had five non-executive members who were up for re-election annually at the annual general meeting (AGM) (see Figure 9.1).

Heath had been chairman of the company since January 2001. This 'semi-retirement' role was a fitting conclusion to a long and successful career. Brought up in a well-off family, he had been educated at the best colleges, gained significant international experience in a well-known multinational and even spent three years in the Foreign Office. 'I didn't build my career on being aggressive or proffering my advice', Heath reflected, trying to understand why Simon was opposed to his ideas. As he reviewed their interactions over the year, he could see that tensions between them would continue to grow.

From bad to worse

20 January 2002

Heath's lunch with his predecessor took a disappointing turn. He could not discuss his concerns about Simon's behaviour. The retired chairman's advice was simple:

> Let Simon run the show, his track record is unmatched – headhunters for the 'bulge bracket' companies of our nation are watching him closely. We have to be careful that we don't lose him. Just support Simon and enjoy your job.

Then the conversation turned to cars and politics. At least Heath now knew that he could not expect much support from the two longest-serving members on the board. They were old buddies of his predecessor and had been on the board for more than ten years. The three kept close contact in the 'old boy network'.

3 February 2002

At the board meeting, Heath and Simon clashed openly. Simon bluntly brushed aside a proposal from Dale, a banking executive who had joined the board at the same time as Heath, calling it 'too analytical and not applicable to our business'. Heath and Dale were more embarrassed by Simon's tone and body language than his words. However, the proposal could not have been completely irrelevant. At least CFO Silver had cautiously expressed interest before Simon trashed the idea. Heath forced Simon into a half-hearted apology, but the mood remained tense for the rest of the meeting, despite another year of double-digit growth, profits and earnings – the board should have been in a cheerful mood instead.

28 February 2002

Heath had another heated debate with Simon while preparing the meeting prior to the AGM in April. Heath felt obliged to propose some improvements in corporate governance and to increase reporting transparency. He suggested:

- Forming audit, nomination and remuneration committees with only external board members;
- A formal evaluation of the performance of the entire board, including the CEO, COO and CFO; and
- More detailed reporting by business unit and geography.

Simon opposed the ideas, arguing that this would create bureaucracy, impede quick decision making and make the share price more volatile, since dents in individual unit performance could push the stock market in the wrong direction. At the end of the argument, Heath ran out of patience: 'You run the company, I run the board', he told Simon and stormed out of the corporate dining room.

However, Simon's resistance motivated Heath to consult Elicore's six biggest shareholders. Most of them were institutional investors, who held more than 40% of the stocks and who had proposed him as chairman of the board. The group agreed that Heath should discuss the idea of improving corporate governance to meet 'best practice' in his opening speech at the AGM. Later on the board could work out the details. Simon took a conciliatory approach when Heath told him about the shareholder resolution: 'Let's sit down together and work this out', he said, 'I don't think that we fundamentally disagree.' 'How charming he can be, if he wants to', Heath thought.

17 April 2002

The days leading up to the AGM were filled with rumours that Elicore was facing a hostile takeover bid by its larger rival, which had recently been troubled by leadership problems. According to one rumour, the main shareholder of the rival company intended to make Simon the new CEO of the merged company. At the evening meeting before the AGM, originally scheduled to do some routine and last minute tasks, the board informally discussed the idea of a potential merger. No one seemed to be enthusiastic about the idea, but Heath was surprised that Simon did not explain his position with his usual 'bang-bang' clarity. Heath volunteered to communicate to the AGM that the board saw the future of the company in the current framework. Nothing remarkable happened at the AGM, given the great business results. The board was unanimously re-elected.

26 May 2002

Over lunch outside Elicore, Heath met informally with Dale and John Sinclair, who had been on the board for four years, to discuss the new design of corporate governance. When Heath very carefully put out feelers to ascertain opinions on Simon, Sinclair's response was surprising:

> I have observed this guy over time and am shocked by his increasing arrogance. He hasn't listened to the board for nearly two years. If he doesn't listen to us, whom will he listen to?

Dale supported him:

> I have seen this time and again: When executives are very successful they begin to be detached. Normally that is the beginning of their downfall – and the longer they have been successful, the more they take the whole company down with them.

Heath tried to balance his response by sharing their concerns, but also stressing Simon's leadership qualities. However, they agreed on the need to challenge Simon more – and that the appropriate tool was the board performance evaluation.

4 July 2002

While reading the incoming results of the second quarter in his home office, Heath discovered by chance that the earnings had been calculated differently. Although this was probably legal, it was not in line with Elicore's long-standing accounting tradition. A back-of-the-envelope calculation convinced Heath that without the accounting revision, Elicore would not have had double-digit growth. He called the CFO, but Silver was very guarded:

'It was Simon's decision. Please discuss this matter with him', he said drily.

Heath's telephone conversation with Simon escalated into a shouting match. Simon threatened to hold Heath accountable for any negative developments in the stock price; Heath finally accused Simon of 'cooking the books' and threatened to bring the matter to the attention of the whole board and to propose that they did 'not sign off the second quarter results'. Then he hung up. An hour later Silver called and proposed solving the issue by asking the auditors to give their professional opinion on the accounting change. Silver told Heath that this was what he had proposed to Simon after Simon had told him about the clash. 'He was pretty upset, but agreed', Silver told Heath, who then also agreed. Personally he was happy that they had avoided a shootout.

The auditor came up with another proposal, which was more in line with Elicore's tradition and just made 'double digits'. Heath called Samuel Rosenstil, who had the most accounting experience on the board. Rosenstil had been brought in during the turnaround, to use this knowledge in the clean up. However, he had always been more cautious than Simon, and had become increasingly silent. Rosenstil was not happy:

> We have piled up huge risks with the accelerated growth strategy – and now we are trying to avoid the consequences by a change in accounting. But nobody listens to me anyhow. If these accounting tricks continue, I will resign pretty soon.

Heath could not help telling him that at the next board meeting he would propose the changes in corporate governance in detail.

> You have my word this will increase our proactive involvement, and in particular any changes in accounting rules will have to be approved by the audit committee.

With this assurance, Rosenstil gave his blessing to the accounting changes proposed by the auditors.

Pressing questions

Heath was convinced that Elicore needed to improve its corporate governance processes. He was confident about the consultant's proposal and also about his own instincts. The board meeting would be the ideal opportunity to discuss everything.

But could he have avoided the deterioration of his relations with Simon? Would the CEO really resign or would he fight? Heath knew Simon could command the vote of the COO and of the two longest-serving board members, which – including himself – amounted to four out of the nine votes. Heath could probably count on the other three non-executives as well as the CFO, but he could not be 100% sure. Simon probably knew that Heath had a small majority. But should Heath really take the risk of splitting the board? Was his proposal too far-reaching? Should he make a last attempt to seek a compromise, if not reconciliation?

And, last but not least, if the board agreed on the changes, how would the stock market receive the news of the corporate governance changes? How could he explain them? Heath had to find answers, quick.

Q: How do you see the relationship between the CEO and the board, here represented by the chairman?

A: There needs to be a balance between the role of management and the role of the board. Whether you have a separation between the chairman and the CEO, which is clearly the practice in Europe, or whether you have a combination in the US with a lead director, you need a clear separation between governance and management. The biggest risk in combining the roles is when you have a CEO who dominates the board. That's clearly what Mr Simon is trying to do and it is totally unacceptable. Heath needs to stand up to him. The evaluation that Simon is resisting is routine practice. The board's job, especially the non-executive directors, is to evaluate the CEO. If the CEO is resisting evaluation, it indicates that he is trying to protect himself from something. That's a sign of real insecurity. My view is they should stand up to him and call his bluff on resigning.

Q: But would this not raise the risk of a split board?

A: In terms of Heath counting votes on the board, this raises questions about inside directors having votes on these matters. I think you want to watch how many inside directors you have. I totally disagree with Heath's predecessor when he says, 'Let Simon run the show.' That's not doing your job as chairman of the board. A lot of companies got into trouble, by letting a visibly successful CEO run the company into the ground. Look at the ABB case, they let a very powerful CEO dominate the board and do some things that were totally inappropriate. So Heath has to stand up and unite the independent directors.

Q: What do you think about the argument of creating too much bureaucracy?

A: I don't buy it. Heath's proposal is just routine, standard stuff that you have to do. The board's most important job is to evaluate the CEO and to decide whether that CEO should continue. There's no excuse for not doing it. These procedures are not at all bureaucratic. This is just your job. The CEO reports to the board and he cannot ride roughshod over the board like this. This case is set in 2002, at a time when everyone was challenging corporate governance. At Novartis we created a new corporate governance committee in October 2001 because we felt that European companies really need to look at their governance, otherwise they are going to end up like Swissair and ABB. Heath is on solid ground in creating governance procedures such as committees and evaluation of CEO, COO and CFO separately. At one point he tells Simon, 'You run the company, I run the board.' That's correct. Heath has to make sure that he has a majority of the board behind him. And that is the problem: there are these board members who aren't stepping up to their responsibilities. If they don't, there will be a problem.

Q: What do you think about an 'executive session' of independent directors only?

A: Simon would never permit his board to meet without his presence. My reaction to that was, 'That's not his call.' The board has to stand up to him and say that they are going to meet without him. It's now law in the United States that you have to do that. I think it's a good law. Let Simon run the company, but not the board.

Q: How important is the CEO as a person?

A: The CEO is just one person, and organizations are made up of many people. Good CEOs build up a team around them so they're dispensable. CEOs who try to say they're indispensable – this is a misnomer created by the stock market. CEOs are just one employee among many, and have to be a little more modest about their roles. The CEO needs to be very respectful of the board members because they are his bosses. If I were Heath, I would consider asking Simon to resign. It's time for a CEO who is more of a team builder. When you've had these imperial CEOs, the results in the long term are not good.

Case study: National Life: Stay and fight or vote with your feet?

Dennis Miller bit his lip. He looked around the table, but seemed to be the only one who had noticed. Once again, Mike Stewart, Chairman and CEO of National Life, had completely ignored his contribution and moved on to the last item on the board agenda – the upcoming annual general meeting (AGM).

> Does anybody *not* want to stand for re-election to the board?

Stewart surveyed the assembled board members and his gaze finally came to rest on Miller. 'What am I doing here?' Miller asked himself. But on second thoughts, the successful software entrepreneur felt a sense of obligation:

I have never run away when things got tough. I have accepted the mandate, and I have to stay and fight.

But what were his options for success? What could he as an individual board member do to shake up this change-resistant company? What was his real obligation? Who could be an ally?

National Life

National Life was the number two insurer. It had a strong hold in towns with populations less than 100 000 due to the strength of its tight agent network, regarded as one of the most powerful, if expensive, sales machines. National Life had added Property&Casualty insurance to its portfolio several years earlier and had recently added asset management, but its funds were not top performers. The company was very stable in every aspect. The agents achieved a high customer retention rate. Products and services changed as slowly as the turnover of the board – the average service was more than ten years. 'The most important asset in insurance is reliability', was Stewart's deep conviction. National Life was not an outperformer in its industry, but it had not experienced any severe troubles either. Ownership was widely fragmented: four institutional investors held more than 10%, the rest was owned by individuals as a 'widow-and-orphan paper', a secure stock with a continual stream of dividends.

National Life's board had 13 members, most of them in their late 50s/early 60s, apart from the younger powerful sales boss, Jim Allen – who clearly had ambitions to succeed Stewart – and former chairman and CEO, Steve Bryan – who was in his 70s. Miller had been brought on to the board to tip the balance in favour of 'non-executive' members. This was, however, rather euphemistic because three of the eight 'non-execs' were former corporate officers and not inclined to challenge their former colleagues. Only Bryan still seemed to exert a considerable level of influence behind the scenes. The five corporate executives on the board were under Stewart's tight control – he was the unchallenged boss. National Life had no formal evaluation in place – either for the CEO/chairman or for the directors on the board.

Miller and one other board member, Carlos Sekujan, a banker, had to fly in for the meetings; all the others lived within driving distance of the headquarters. Despite this closeness, the non-executive board members had little contact with each other outside the eight board meetings per year. It was also not customary to seek direct contact with National Life employees, customers or other outside parties.

Finding a place in an established board

Living on the West Coast and married to a famous novelist, 38-year-old Miller was indeed the 'odd-one-out' in this circle of older men. He had his own IT business, which was booming despite the technology bear market. The artificial intelligence on which his special program relied identified patterns of money laundering and other dubious financial transactions in the millions of transactions on the global financial markets. Because of new security legislation, many companies – not just financial service institutions – were eager to install his software.

Miller's first interactions with the board went well – socially. Everybody was interested in his career and his wife and asked a lot of questions over lunch. In the meetings he asked only one or two, more factual, questions; otherwise he listened and tried to learn about and understand National

Life's business model. He felt that there was not much time for discussion anyhow, since more than half of the time was spent on issues for which information and decisions by the board were required for regulatory reasons. Miller never understood the deeper logic of all this – except that one older colleague explained to him: 'When something goes wrong, the regulators know whom to sue.' The rest of the time was filled with presentations and a couple of questions afterwards. Everybody seemed to be happy with the routine of meeting early in the morning and finishing with a good lunch in the executive dining room.

Miller remembered only two interactions with board members outside the board meetings: Bryan, who had proposed him for the board, had invited Miller to dinner the evening before his second meeting. He tried to explain a bit about the history, culture and business of National Life and gave him some background information on some of the people on the board. Bryan was a 'Grand Seigneur' and Miller enjoyed the evening with him. The other occasion was when he and Sekujan happened to be on the same flight home after the memorable fifth board meeting.

The fifth board meeting: a watershed

At this meeting, a so-called IT strategy was on the agenda. As usual, a board file arrived a couple of days before the meeting. Due to time pressure, Miller read the proposals only on the way to the meeting. They seemed to be merely a costly extension of the existing mainframe, which Miller thought to be slow, expensive and too centralized to allow quick access to relevant information from every part of the organization. In particular, the proposed system was not capable of serving customers online, neither for information nor anything close to 'e-business'. Because of the legacy systems, Miller assumed that several interfaces still had to be bridged by entering data manually.

Immediately after the presenter, a technical expert in his mid-50s, had finished his talk, Miller explained that he 'really didn't get it'. After finishing his passionate five-minute intervention, he suddenly noticed the disbelief in the eyes of his colleagues. Into the silence, Allen said coldly:

> Please note that we are not in financial services, but in insurance, and I don't let my agents become victims of the latest fleeting fashion. We have seen where this has landed our competitors.

Miller was perplexed, but hit back angrily, 'If you are not able to manage different sales channels, you will be out of business pretty soon.' Stewart stepped in, 'I think our IT people have done a great job in the past and will continue to do so in the future.' Miller was desperate – after all, he had been brought to the board because of his IT background: 'On the contrary, from what I can see, National Life is an absolute laggard in IT. You will have to go through a massive renewal process, not just some extensions, to stay competitive.' Stewart went red in the face, but kept his cool. 'Thank you for your opinion. I don't see any further intervention, so we'll proceed to the next item.'

Miller slumped in his seat. He knew he was right, but he knew also that he had made a mistake. Bryan's words came to mind: 'Never challenge Stewart in public' and 'Nobody at National Life likes surprises.' But it was too late. And from then on, Stewart consistently ignored Miller's input.

The lunch was over more quickly than usual, with only minimal small talk. Miller realized, 'Now I am an outsider.' On the way back, Sekujan was not particularly inclined to talk to him. But Sekujan's parting words as he took his first-class seat on the plane – before Miller made his way to the economy section – were:

> Remember, they invited you on to the board to do business with them, not to offend them.

Fall from grace

At the next board meeting Miller did not hesitate to give his opinion on different items on the agenda. However, Stewart ignored him completely. While the meeting continued, Miller continued to ponder his options. Could he have avoided the situation? Was it too late to repair the relationship? Could Bryan serve as a mediator? Or, failing this, he thought defiantly:

> But I can also live happily as a maverick in this circle. Or if I approach the institutional shareholders, we could probably organize enough pressure to replace all the executives, except Bryan. Then there would be six non-executives on the board, who should have no reservations in challenging executive management.

Or would it all just be a big waste of his time?

Q: Is Miller's situation on the board a typical one?

A: This happens all the time with independent directors. You get them on the board and then you don't want their opinions. It's a big problem in corporate governance in Europe and the US. Miller felt like he was not part of the club. I know a number of other board members who have resigned from boards because they felt like they were 'odd man out', not part of the club. A clubby board is not a good thing. This smells like Swissair.

Q: What was Miller's mistake?

A: Miller didn't know how to handle himself in a boardroom. He was a bit impertinent, a bit aggressive. Nevertheless, he had that responsibility and he was speaking from his area of expertise, which was information technology. Miller wasn't very diplomatic. However, he had a right to raise questions and the management had a responsibility to give answers. The board should not have tried to push him out. Serving on a board shouldn't be for social reasons. Having said that, maybe he didn't have as keen an understanding of the application of information technology in this industry. I've seen that at Medtronic where board members tried to apply their knowledge of technology to Medtronic and I invited them to spend time with the management to gain an understanding of how the technology applied because it is different in each business. You can't just say, 'Your guys are behind.' Maybe they're taking a different approach. There are much better ways to handle this.

Q: What could be done?

A: It's up to the board to ask the management to do a study. And then perhaps to ask Mr Miller to spend time evaluating the study and make a recommendation to the board since this is his area of expertise.

Q: Should Miller stay on the board?

A: If the board doesn't want his expertise, he should move on. It is totally inappropriate to approach the institutional shareholders. That would destroy the organization and a disagreement over information technology is not worth it. This is strictly a board issue. The independent board members need to stand up and ask for a meeting and executive session without the CEO. That's just the way you run a board.

Q: Is there any chance for Miller to find redress?

A: In this case, there is a combined chairman and CEO, but no lead director. There is no balance between the power of the chairman and CEO. Is there another lead director to balance the power? The predecessor, Bryan, is too old: he should get off the board. There is a real problem not having a lead director.

References

Byrne, J.A. (2000) 'The Best and the Worst Boards', *Business Week*, 24 January 2000: 152.

Boyle, M. (2001) 'The Dirty Half-Dozen: America's Worst Boards', *Fortune*, 14 May 2001: 249–252.

Carter, C.B. and J.W. Lorsch (2003) *Back to the Drawing Board: Designing Corporate Boards for a Complex World*, Boston, Mass.: Harvard Business School Press.

Chakravarthy, B. and P. Lorange (2004) *Leading for Growth*. Forthcoming.

Dotlich, D.L. and Peter Cairo (2003) *Why CEOs Fail*, San Francisco, CA: Jossey-Bass.

Finkelstein, S. (2003) *Why Smart Executives Fail*, London: Portfolio/Penguin.

George, W.W. (2001) 'It's Time to Improve Corporate Governance', *Directors & Boards*, Vol. 25, Iss. 2: 23–28.

George, W.W. (2002) 'Imbalance of Power', *Harvard Business Review*, Vol. 80, Iss. 7: 22–23.

George, W. (2003) *Automatic Leadership*, San Francisco, CA: Jossey-Bass.

Hamilton, S. and A.-V. Ohlsson (2000) *Kvaerner Acquires Trafalgar House: Eric Tonseth Leads Kvaerner in Viking Raid*, Lausanne: IMD Case No. IMD-1-0182.

Korn/Ferry International (2001) *28th Annual Board of Directors Study 2001*, Study IV, New York.

Lee, S.-H. and P.H. Plan (2000) 'Competencies of Directors in Global Firms: Requirements for Recruitment and Evaluation', *Corporate Governance – An International Review*, Vol. 8, No. 3: 204.

Lorenzen, J.C. (2000) 'Bestyrelsens Rolle og Hovedoppgaver', Speech, Copenhagen.

Lorsch, J.W. (1995) 'Empowering in the Board', *Harvard Business Review*, Vol. 73, Iss. 1: 107–117.

Lorsch, J.W. and E. MacIver (1989) *Pawns or Potentates: The Reality of America's Corporate Boards*, Boston, MA: Harvard Business School Press.

McNulty, T. and A. Pettigrew (1999) 'Strategists on the Board', *Organization Studies*, Vol. 20, Iss. 1: 47–74.

Neubauer, F. and A.G. Lank (1998) 'The Family Business: Its Governance for Sustainability', London: Macmillan Press Ltd.

Neubauer, F., U. Steger and G. Rädler (1999) 'DaimlerChrysler: The Involvement of the Boards', IMD Case IMD-3-0771, Lausanne: IMD.

Novartis (2001) 'Novartis gibt neue Verwaltungsratsstruktur bekannt', Press release, Basel, 2 November 2001.

OECD (1998) *Corporate Governance, Improving Competitiveness and Access to Capital in Global Markets*, Paris: OECD.

Pearce, J.A. and S.A. Zahra (1991) 'The Relative Power of CEOs and Boards of Directors: Associations with Corporate Performance', *Strategic Management Journal*, Vol. 12, Iss. 2: 135–153.

Regierungskommission Corporate Governance (2001) *Unternehmensführung-Unternehmenskontrolle-Modernisierung des Aktienrechts, Bericht der Regierungskommission 'Corporate Governance' (Report II)*, Frankfurt, July 2001.

Regierungskommission Deutscher Corporate Governance Code (2002) *German Corporate Governance Code*, Berlin.

Salter, M. (2003) 'Notes on Governance and Corporate Control', *Journal of Strategic Management Education*, Vol. 1, No. 1: 5–54.

SpencerStuart (2001) *Board Index 2001*, New York, Chicago (http://www.spencerstuart.com)

Steger, U. and H. Krapf (2002) *War at the Helm of Elicore*, IMD Case IMD-3-1158, Lausanne: IMD.

Steger, U. and H. Krapf (2003) 'Corporate Governance in Global Companies – Content not Structure as the Main Driver', IMD working paper.

Steger, U. and G. Rädler (2003) 'DaimlerChrysler: Corporate Governance Dynamics in a Global Company', IMD Case IMD-3-1273, Lausanne: IMD.

Stopford, J.M. and C.W.F. Baden-Fuller (1990) 'Corporate Rejuvenation', *Journal of Management Studies*, Vol. 27, Iss. 4: 399–415.

Strebel, P. (2003) *Trajectory Management: Leading a Business over Time*, London: Wiley.

Tainio, R., Lilja, K. and T. Santalainen (2001) 'The Role of Boards in Facilitating or Limiting Learning in Organizations', *Handbook of Organizational Learning &*

Knowledge, Dierkes M., Antal, A.B., Child, J. and Nonaka, I. (eds) Oxford: Oxford University Press: 428–445.

Tainio, R. and A. Valpola (ed.) (1996) *A Manager under Conditions of Change*, Porvoo: Werner Söderström OY.

Thornton, E. and L. Lavelle (2002) 'It's Getting Tough to Fill a Boardroom', *BusinessWeek*, 29 July 2002: 34–35.

Wall Street Journal (2003) *The Corporate Scandals of 2002: Cases and Effects*, Explanatory Reporting for the 2003 Pulitzer Prize, NY, NY.

Zahra, S. and J. Pearce (1989) 'Boards of Directors and Corporate Financial Performance: A Review and Integrative Model', *Journal of Management Studies*, Vol. 15, Iss. 2: 291–334.

Notes

Now that Everything is in Place, Does it Matter?

1 The Office of the Federal Register informs citizens of their rights and obligations by providing ready access to the official texts of Federal laws, Presidential documents, administrative regulations and notices and descriptions of Federal organizations, programmes and activities. (http://www.archives.gov/federal_register/about/mission.html)

How can Corporate Governance Fail?

1 For a more detailed account of the events and the corporate governance structure see the IMD case study 3–1057, *Grounding: Did Corporate Governance Fail at Swissair?* At times the company was officially called SAirGroup, but for the convenience of the reader we stay here with the popular name Swissair.
2 Feeder airlines bring passengers from outlying communities to larger airports.
3 Two-tier boards, prominently in the German speaking areas of Scandinavia and optional in France, separate legally the supervising function from the management function. Both the supervisory board and the management board have legally described duties and responsibilities, which are detailed in the Articles of Association. No cross-membership is allowed. One-tier boards, the Anglo-Saxon model, combine executive and non-executives officers in one board with no legal separations of their duties.

Shedding Some Light into the Black Box

1 The consensus-based German-style economic structure, often known as the 'social market economy', is often contrasted with the more freewheeling British and American system.

Managing Complexity in Global Corporate Governance

1 For the official description see DaimlerChrysler's Annual Report 2002, pp. 150–155. Our focus here is not on legal issues, but rather on the decision-making dynamic.

The Role and Responsibilities of the CEO

1. I am thankful to Jens Christian Lorenzen for helpful inputs to this chapter (see also Lorenzen, 2000).
2. Transportation or loading and unloading of cargo using a flat-bottomed barge, or lighter.

Performance Evaluation of Corporate Boards and Boards of Directors

1 See our list of Further Readings for further argumentation by some authors.
2 See OECD (1998, p. 50). The text of many corporate governance codes is available from the World Bank's Internet site on Principles of Best Corporate Governance Practice: www.worldbank.org/html/fpd/privatesector/cg/codes.html
3 See Regierungskommission Corporate Governance (2001).
4 See Regierungskommission Deutscher Corporate Governance Code (2002, p. 11).

5 See Byrne (2000) and Boyle (2001).

6 See SpencerStuart (2001, p. 13).

7 See Korn/Ferry International (2001, p. 6).

8 See George (2002, pp. 22–23).

9 See Lee and Plan (2000).

10 See SpencerStuart (2001, p. 13).

11 See George (2001, pp. 24–25).

12 See Novartis (2001).

13 See Thornton and Lavelle (2002, p. 35).

Cobra versus Commerzbank, War at the Helm of Elicore, and National Life

1 PriceWaterhouse Coopers (1998) 'The Cost of Non-Europe in Financial Services'. *Research on the Cost of Non-Europe: Basic Findings*, Vol. 9, Brussels: European Union.

Index

Note: Figures and Tables are indicated by *italic page numbers*